The Bunner Sisters

By Richard Alleman

Inspired by a novella by Edith Wharton

PRODUCTION HISTORY

The Bunner Sisters, by Richard Alleman, premiered at the A.C.T. Costume Shop theatre in San Francisco, February 11 to 21, 2016. Produced by RE:ACT; artistic director Josiah Polhemus. Directed by Anthony Newfield; setting and lighting by Jessica Bertine; costumes by Chanterelle Grover; sound design by William Myers; production stage manager: Rena Lourie. The cast was as follows:

ANN ELIZA BUNNER: Amy Prosser
EVELINA BUNNER: Heather Kellogg
MRS MELLINS: Anne Buelteman
MRS LEOPOLD GOLDFARB: Tara Blau
MR HERMAN RAMY/PRIEST: Josiah Polhemus

THE BUNNER SISTERS

CHARACTERS

ANN ELIZA BUNNER. 40 years old; a seamstress

EVELINA BUNNER. 29 years old; her sister

MRS MELLINS. 50 to 60; their upstairs neighbor; a seamstress

MRS LEOPOLD GOLDFARB. 50; a wealthy customer

MR HERMAN RAMY. Early- to mid-40s; a German clocksmith

A PRIEST. (played by same actor who plays Mr. Ramy)

TIME AND PLACE

The entire action of the play takes place from 1888 through 1889 in the Bunner Sisters' basement shop/living quarters in lower Manhattan

ACT I

SCENE 1

The house lights dim and fade to black, as we hear a cacophony of city sounds suggesting 1880s New York—streetcar bells, clanging trolleys, the clip-clop of horses, the voices of hawkers. The street sounds crescendo, then fade, but don't disappear entirely, as the lights come up to reveal the stage divided into two distinct areas. Stage left is the Bunner Sisters' basement shop and work area. Upstage a door with a glass window on the top half leads to the outside; a small display window left of the door holds artificial flowers and bands of scalloped fabrics. Inside the shop, a central work table is set with three stools. The space also has a free-standing full-length mirror, a dressmaker's mannequin, a pedal-powered sewing machine, plus various tables and shelves displaying additional bands of fabric, ribbons, and fringes. Separated by a velvet curtain, the stage-right area is the sisters' living quarters. A bed with a brass headstand is down right; a round dining table with three chairs is center; and, further upstage, a hutch—with shelves above and a cabinet below—holds dishes, tea things, glasses, silverware, and decanters. On the top shelf is a porcelain figurine of a grand lady in an elaborate ruffled dress and towering wig.

As the lights come up full, we find ANN ELIZA BUNNER, a plain woman who looks older than her 40 years, at the work table in the shop, carefully gift-wrapping a large nickel-plated clock. She wears spectacles, a long black skirt, and a white blouse. When she finishes wrapping the clock, she turns over a sign on the door to indicate that the shop is closed, then goes into the living area, where she slips on a slightly worn black-silk jacket, which she anchors with a mosaic broach. She then returns to the shop area and checks her appearance in the full-length mirror. She plays with her hair and satisfied, though not necessarily pleased, with how she looks, goes back into the living quarters, where she withdraws a cut-glass decanter from the cabinet along with several small crystal glasses, which she sets on the table. She next moves a small vase of fresh flowers from atop the cabinet and puts it on the table as well. As she arranges the table, she is interrupted by the clang of the doorbell. Peeved that a customer is calling when the store is closed, she nonetheless goes into the shop to see who it is. When she sees that it's MRS LEOPOLD GOLDFARB, her mood lifts as she opens the door. MRS GOLDFARB is dressed in a fashionable suit, notable for its puffed sleeves, and a stylish feather-trimmed hat. She carries a large brocaded bag.

ANN ELIZA: Oh, Mrs. Goldfarb. I didn't expect—I haven't seen you in months.

MRS GOLDFARB: I know, darling. We've been abroad and just got back a few days ago. I'm so sorry to disturb you. I know it's late, but I saw a light, so I took a chance.

ANN ELIZA: Please. How can I help you?

MRS GOLDFARB: *(taking a flat tissue paper-wrapped package out of her bag and unwrapping it to reveal a shimmery evening dress)* It's this. It's one of my favorite frocks and I'd adore to wear it Friday evening to the Christine Nilsson recital at the Academy—but the sleeves...you see, we've just come from Paris and puffed sleeves *(indicating her suit jacket)* like these are all the rage. So I'm wondering if you might redo the sleeves on this one? Give them *un peu de* "puff"!

ANN ELIZA: Let's have a look. *(examining MRS GOLDFARB'S sleeve)* Ummm....it's a little complicated, but if I can't do something, I'm sure Evelina can. I always say she can take a pattern with just her eye.

MRS GOLDFARB: You don't have to tell me. Those bonnets she did for me were quite a hit in London. Oh, and here (*taking a magazine from her bag*), I brought this—it's a journal *de la mode*, from Paris. I've marked all the puffed sleeves.

ANN ELIZA: That will be a big help. Thank you, Mrs. Goldfarb.

MRS GOLDFARB: Now, I mustn't keep you any longer. It looks like you're dressed to go out. (*pointing to Ann Eliza's silk jacket*) Lovely fabric—

ANN ELIZA: Oh, it's just my old sacramental black silk. We ain't going out though—but it is a special occasion. Evelina's birthday.

MRS GOLDFARB: Where are you celebrating?

ANN ELIZA: (*slightly embarrassed*) Why, here. It's only a small affair. Just me, Evelina, and Mrs. Mellins, the dressmaker who lives upstairs.

MRS GOLDFARB: Oh yes. I've used her. A good seamstress but, well, not nearly as...creative...as the two of you.

ANN ELIZA: (*embarrassed*) Oh...well...

MRS GOLDFARB: (*moving toward the door*) No need to tell her that, of course (*winks*).

ANN ELIZA: Of course not. Come by Thursday and we'll seewhere we are with your sleeves. (*seeing MRS MELLINS outside the door, as she goes to open it*) Why, this would be Mrs. Mellins now.

MRS MELLINS enters; she is a small woman well into her

fifties; her hair bristles with imitation tortoise shell pins—and she wears a good half dozen metal bangles on each of her wrists. There is an awkward moment as MRS MELLINS enters and MRS GOLDFARB leaves.

ANN ELIZA: You know Mrs. Goldfarb, I believe.

MRS MELLINS: Yes. Good evening, Madam.

MRS GOLDFARB: Yes, hello. (*to Ann Eliza*) And goodbye. Hope I haven't disturbed you too much. Oh, and do have a lovely party. My best wishes to your sister.

ANN ELIZA: Thank you. I'll tell Evelina.

MRS GOLDFARB: *Au revoir*…as they say in Paris.

ANN ELIZA (*closing the door*) I didn't know she was coming. I had already closed the shop when she dropped by.

MRS MELLINS: Just like the Jews—always want special service.

ANN ELIZA: (*slipping MRS GOLDFARB'S dress onto the mannequin down left*) She's a good customer—and a lovely woman. I don't care what her religion is.

MRS MELLINS: But you can't trust 'em.

ANN ELIZA: A lot of people say that about Catholics. All your mumbo-jumbo.

MRS MELLINS: Speaking of which, I heard they arrested that negro woman who lives down the block for having some kind of weird witchcraft ceremonies.

ANN ELIZA: What?

MRS MELLINS: They was killing chickens and drinking the blood—right here on this street. But it wasn't the noise that got the neighbors all upset—it was all them headless chickens running around the hallways.

ANN ELIZA: Stop. I don't believe a word of it. Just another one of your stories from the *Police Gazette.*

MRS MELLINS: It's the god's truth. Mr. Walker, the butcher in the Stuyvesant Market—he lives in the building and he swears it happened. Anyway, they took that old negra down to the station house and she ain't been seen or heard from since. And according to Mr. Walker, nobody from his building has bought any meat for almost a week—but they've been eating chicken every day!

ANN ELIZA: Ah, your stories, Mrs. Mellins! You should write for one of them crazy newspapers you read.

MRS MELLINS: (*eying the package on the work table*) Where's the birthday girl?

ANN ELIZA: She's delivering them flounces we've been working on for the last week.

MRS MELLINS: (*indicating the package, as ANN ELIZA takes it into the living quarters and puts it on the top shelf of the hutch*) And what would that be?

ANN ELIZA: A clock. A nickel clock. Evelina's been wanting one for years. Now she won't have to run round the corner to the Square every morning, rain or shine, to see what time it is.

MRS MELLINS: (*now leafing through MRS GOLDFARB'S journal de la mode*) I hate to think what it must a cost you.

ANN ELIZA: I've been saving up from some little jobs I took, so I could finally get her one.

MRS MELLINS: Well, I hope nobody ever gives me one of them things. A big clock like that would only remind me I'm that much closer to judgment day.

ANN ELIZA: Oh, go on!

MRS MELLINS: So where did you get your time machine?

ANN ELIZA: Over near the Stuyvesant Market in this little shop I ain't never seen before. Seems it's only been there a few months. As you know, I let most of the shopping and delivering to Evelina.

MRS MELLINS: Yes. I don't know why you like staying inside all the time.

ANN ELIZA: Somebody's got to look after the shop—and Evelina don't know how to treat the customers. Besides, she likes to go out, dress up a little, put a flower in her hair.

MRS MELLINS: (*mischievously*) And we all know why she does that.

ANN ELIZA: Don't start, Mrs. Mellins.

MRS MELLINS: You know as well as I. She's looking to catch herself a gentleman. And she ain't getting any younger. How long since that Sunday school teacher used to come by?

ANN ELIZA: Maybe six months now—but that ain't why she goes out. She's just more adventurous than me.

MRS MELLINS: That's what you think. Anyway, what about your clock?

ANN ELIZA: Well, I thought I'd have to go up to Stern's on 23rd Street—and then, like magic, right before my eyes, there was this nice little shop right on 15th. With the nicest shopkeeper, a German gentleman named Herman Ramy. I don't think he's been here all that long—still has an accent. And he used to work for Tiff'ny's.

MRS MELLINS: How old is he?

ANN ELIZA: Oh, I don't know. Maybe 40—a little more, a little less.

MRS MELLINS: Is he married?

ANN ELIZA: Well, I'm sure I don't know. Really!

MRS MELLINS: Was he wearing a ring?

ANN ELIZA: I....can't remember (*she can; he wasn't*).

MRS MELLINS: Ummmm...

ANN ELIZA: He was just a nice polite man—and I guess I felt a little sorry for him...something about his eyes—he had a sort of lonely look (*she stops and shudders for an instant—a feeling has come over her that she's not familiar with*)...

MRS MELLINS: What is it, Ann Eliza?

ANN ELIZA: Nuttin'. He...he give me a very good price.

MRS MELLINS: Well, it sure seems he made quite an impression on you.

ANN ELIZA: Don't be silly. He was just real polite. Like I said—a gentleman.

MRS MELLINS: Perhaps you should introduce him to Evelina—if he ain't married...and he's lonely.

ANN ELIZA: Ah, your silliness, Mrs. Mellins. Come, help me with the cake. Evelina will be back any minute.

MRS MELLINS gets up to join ANN ELIZA at the hutch. At the same time, we see the front door open and EVELINA BUNNER enter. Dangerously close to 30 years old, she is wearing a plaid coat and a matching bonnet. She looks around the shop, takes off her coat and hat, and heads towards the living quarters.

EVELINA: Hello?

ANN ELIZA: Back here!

ANN ELIZA and MRS MELLINS have lit a candle on a small cake. They hold it up to EVELINA as she enters the space.

ANN ELIZA and MRS MELLINS: (*singing*) Happy Birthday to You; Happy Birthday to You; Happy Birthday, Evelina. Happy Birthday to You!

EVELINA blows out the candle, then hugs MRS MELLINS and ANN ELIZA, who gives her the wrapped clock.

EVELINA: Why, thank you!

EVELINA takes the present and begins opening it.

MRS MELLINS: So what did you wish for?

ANN ELIZA: She mustn't tell you—she won't get it.

MRS MELLINS: She don't have to tell me. I have a pretty good hunch.

ANN ELIZA gives MRS MELLINS a look as EVELINA finishes opening the present.

EVELINA: Look!...Oh, thank you, Ann Eliza. It's beautiful—and listen, it's ticking! And it's the right time, too.

ANN ELIZA: And we only have to wind it every two days—it's the latest mechanism. From Germany.

She picks up the clock and puts it on the shelf next to the figurine of the grand lady.

MRS MELLINS: And she got it from the nicest man—also from Germany!

ANN ELIZA: Mrs. Mellins—please!

MRS MELLINS: Straight off the boat!

EVELINA: What is she talking about?

ANN ELIZA: She's talking nonsense—as usual.

MRS MELLINS: Very handsome—with beautiful eyes. But she won't tell you who he is, because he's her secret friend.

ANN ELIZA: Mr. Ramy ain't nuttin' of the sort.

MRS MELLINS: And it looks like he ain't married.

ANN ELIZA: We don't know that. (*getting angry*) Now, for the last time, Mrs. Mellins, I ask you to stop your silliness.

EVELINA: No, don't stop.

MRS MELLINS: You could always ask him to tea.

EVELINA: Oh, could we, Ann Eliza?

ANN ELIZA: Absolutely not. It would be way too forward. Anyway, we'll probably never see the poor gentleman again.

MRS MELLINS: I think you're wrong about that, Ann Eliza. I predict you're going to see him very soon.

ANN ELIZA: What do you mean?

MRS MELLINS: Listen!

EVELINA: What?

MRS MELLINS: The clock.

ANN ELIZA: Yes?

MRS MELLINS: It's stopped.

*The three women look at the clock, then at one another.
Rather than anger or frustration, all seem to sense some
strange opportunity heralded by the broken timepiece. The
lights fade out to the sound of a slowly ticking clock.*

SCENE 2

*The next morning, around 8:00 A.M. EVELINA is seated at
the table in the living quarters, decorating a hat with artificial
flowers. Sitting next to her, ANN ELIZA is sewing a button
onto a long black coat. The clock, now wrapped in brown
paper, is on the worktable in the shop.*

ANN ELIZA: I'm sure glad you noticed that missing button,
sister. See anything else needs attended to?

EVELINA: Naw, but you outta get rid of that old thing—how
long is it you had it?

ANN ELIZA: Oh probably 20 years—but since I don't go out
that much, it's practically new.

EVELINA: But it looks so old fashioned.

ANN ELIZA: (*getting up, putting on coat*) I'll leave the
fancy dressing to you, sister. This coat has got a lot of years
left in her—and besides, Mr. Ram—

EVELINA: What?

ANN ELIZA: Uh...Mr. Ramy—and everybody else round the
Square—ain't gonna notice what kind a coat I'm wearing, as
long as it's neat and clean.

She looks at herself in the mirror.

EVELINA: Well, at least let me do something to spruce it up. Come over here for a second, Ann Eliza.

EVELINA picks several artificial flowers from a basket beside her and fashions a miniature bouquet, which she pins onto the lapel of ANN ELIZA'S coat.

EVELINA: There—now that's sure to impress your Mr. Ramy.

ANN ELIZA: I wish you'd get it out of your head that I'm trying to impress anybody. *(looking again in the mirror)* But it's real pretty what you done, Evelina. Thank you. Now, I'd better get going. *(getting her hat)* When you finish with Miss Taylor's hat there, we have to start in on them sleeves for Mrs. Goldfarb. And if any customers come in and want to talk to me, tell 'em I'll be back in an hour or so.

EVELINA: *(getting up, moving into the* shop) I don't know why you just don't let me take the clock back, sister.

ANN ELIZA: No, you couldn't find the shop. It's such a small place and besides Mr. Ramy wouldn't know who you are.

EVELINA: He don't have to know me—as long as I got the clock.

ANN ELIZA: That's what I mean—he might think you stole it.

EVELINA: I think you just don't want me to meet him.

ANN ELIZA: Don't be silly. I just don't want to confuse the poor man.

Before EVELINA can reply, there is a wild clanging of the front doorbell and the hysterical cry of a woman trying to get in. ANN ELIZA opens the door to MRS MELLINS.

ANN ELIZA: Well, Mrs. Mellins, what in God's name?

MRS MELLINS: You gotta come up—right now. It's Mrs. Hawkins.

ANN ELIZA: Yes?

MRS MELLINS: Her water's broke...and little Betsy ain't come back with the midwife yet and...you gotta help—I know you pretty much delivered her twins. They har'ly didn't need a midwife.

EVELINA: And with me, too—and the two what died before me.

ANN ELIZA: All right, all right. Is there water boiled?

MRS MELLINS: I think Johnny's started to, but the stove ain't that hot.

ANN ELIZA: Didn't nobody put any more coal on?

MRS MELLINS: I don't know—but...

ANN ELIZA: Do they have towels?

MRS MELLINS: I don't know; I think so.

ANN ELIZA gathers some surplus fabric from a stack in the shop and heads toward the door.

ANN ELIZA: You'd think that after six babies they'd be prepared—

EVELINA: Can I help, too?

ANN ELIZA: No, you stay here and mind the shop.

She exits.

MRS MELLINS: I'll keep you company, dearie. I don't like all that mess upstairs. Just the sight of blood makes me dizzy.

EVELINA: Oh, me too. I don't know how Ann Eliza can stand it.

MRS MELLINS: Your sister's a tough one.

MRS MELLINS looks around the shop and zeroes in on the dressmaker's mannequin, which holds MRS GOLDFARB'S dress.

MRS MELLINS: *(feeling the fabric)* This must a cost that rich Jewess a pretty penny.

EVELINA: You mean cost her husband.

MRS MELLINS: I know! He's the director of one of the biggest banks in town—but I hear her father's even richer than her husband. He owns half of the tenements down off Delancy Street. So she's got it comin' and goin.'

EVELINA: Well, ain't it always like that? Them what has...gets!

MRS MELLINS sees the clock in its wrappings.

MRS MELLINS: And what do we have here?

EVELINA: Our clock. Ann Eliza was on her way to take it back before you came down.

MRS MELLINS: To her *secret* friend!

EVELINA: I told her I could do it, but she said I wouldn't be able to find his shop.

MRS MELLINS: I'm sure she did. I think your sister wants her secret friend all to herself.

EVELINA: Oh, heavens, Mrs. Mellins. My sister ain't interested in secret friends or nuttin' like that.

MRS MELLINS: So why don't you take it back then? You'd be doing your sister a favor.

EVELINA: You think so? Maybe you're right. She's got a lot of work still this afternoon—it would be one less thing for her to do.

MRS MELLINS: And if I may be so bold as to say, you sometimes pay too much mind to your elder sister. You need to take more advantage of things while you still have your youth. You spend way too much time cooped up in this shop.

EVELINA: That's the way things is.

MRS MELLINS: Only if you let 'em. Your sister may want nuttin' to change—but you ain't your sister. How old did you turn yesterday?

EVELINA: 29.

MRS MELLINS: 29—and you know what comes after that. The clock keeps ticking—even if yours don't.

EVELINA: *(with new resolve)* Where did she say that shop was?

MRS MELLINS: Third Avenue—just off the Square. Ask Mr. Walker at the butcher shop. I bet he can tell you exactly where it is. Them shopkeepers all know each other.

EVELINA: You'll stay till Ann Eliza gets back?

MISS MELINS: Don't you worry, dearie. I have no desire to go up there. But remember—I want a full report when you get back. I want to hear all about this Mr. Ramy.

EVELINA gets her coat and puts it on.

EVELINA: Oh, don't you worry. I'll tell you everything. *(posing, as she adjusts her feathered hat)* My bonnet's becoming, isn't it?

MRS MELLINS: You're jest lovely, Miss Bunner. I bet you'll turn quite a few heads on the Square.

EVELINA: *(taking the clock)* Oh, Mrs. Mellins. You always say such sweet things.

MRS MELLINS: It's the truth. Now, you better get going before she comes back and goes herself.

EVELINA: Oh, thank you, Mrs. Mellins. I'll be back...soon.

She exits. MRS MELLINS looks around the shop, stopping again at MRS GOLDFARB'S dress, then examining some fancy fringe at the sewing machine, which she quickly puts down when she hears ANN ELIZA at the front door.

ANN ELIZA: Well, it's another girl.

MRS MELLINS: Everybody all right?

ANN ELIZA: The midwife got there right after me—and is taking care of everything. She seems healthy. They're gonna name her Sheila—like every other female under the age of five on this block. Where's Evelina?

MRS MELLINS: Oh, she went out.

ANN ELIZA: *(glancing at the work table)* What did she do with the clock?

MRS MELLINS: She just left with it—to take it back to your Mr. Ramy. She wasn't sure how long they'd need you upstairs and, well, she thought she'd do you a favor.

ANN ELIZA: But she ain't got no idea where his shop is—

MRS MELLINS: Oh, she's a clever girl. She'll find it.

ANN ELIZA: And besides, I bought the thing. It ain't right somebody else taking it back.

MRS MELLINS: I don't think it matters all that much.

ANN ELIZA: *(taking off her coat and laying it on the work table)* It don't matter? It matters to me! There's right ways and wrong ways of doing things.

MRS MELLINS: You live with too many rules, Miss Bunner, if you don't mind my sayin' so. Times is changing...it's almost 1890.

ANN ELIZA: We need rules. Otherwise, everything would fall apart. That's why our people left the old country.

MRS MELLINS: I don't know about yours in Germany, but mine left Ireland because they was starving. But let's not get into an argument, Miss Bunner.

ANN ELIZA: You're right, Mrs. Mellins. Not everybody sees eye to eye. And now, I'd better get to work on Mrs. Goldfarb's dress.

MRS MELLINS: Ah, yes. And I guess I'll be goin' back up to the maternity ward. Good day, Miss Bunner.

ANN ELIZA: Good day, Mrs. Mellins.

MRS MELLINS exits the front door. ANN ELIZA, upset, picks up her coat, but before hanging it up, she strips off the spray of artificial flowers that EVELINA pinned on the lapel. She is about to throw them into a trash bin, then pauses and instead deposits them back into a basket on the work table as the lights fade to black and the clock ticks softly..

SCENE 3

7:30 that evening. The sisters have just finished dinner. ANN ELIZA is at the hutch preparing tea, while EVELINA looks admiringly at the clock.

ANN ELIZA: Good gracious, Evelina. I think that clock has you mesmerized.

EVELINA: I just want to make sure she's still running.

ANN ELIZA: Well, can't you hear her ticking?

EVELINA: I can—but I like to watch her up close and see the minute hand actually moving.

ANN ELIZA: Doubting Thomas. He told you she only had a speck of dust in her, didn't he?

EVELINA: (*sitting*) He said he *thought* that's what it was—but he wasn't sure. He said it could be something wrong with the— I forget what you call it. Anyway, he said he'd call round and see, day after tomorrow, after supper.

ANN ELIZA: (*shocked*) He did?

EVELINA: Why, yes.

ANN ELIZA: You're full of surprises sister sometimes. Why didn't you tell me?

EVELINA: You was angry enough at me for taking her back to him.

ANN ELIZA: But we don't har'ly know him.

EVELINA: I think he's real nice, Ann Eliza. And I don't believe he's 40 either; but he does look kinder sick. I guess he's pretty lonesome, all by hisself in that store. (*a beat*) I kinder thought that maybe his saying he'd call round about the clock was just an excuse.

ANN ELIZA: What do you mean?

EVELINA: Well, I don't pretend to be smarter than other folks, but I guess Mr. Herman Ramy wouldn't be sorry to pass an evening here, 'stead of spending it all alone in that pokey little place of his.

ANN ELIZA: I guess he's got plenty of friends of his own.

EVELINA: No, he ain't either. He's got hardly any—

ANN ELIZA: Did he tell you that, too?

EVELINA: Why yes. He seemed to be just crazy to talk to somebody—somebody agreeable, I mean. I think he'd a told me everything ever happened to him if I'd a had the time to stay and listen.

The doorbell clangs.

ANN ELIZA: That would be Mrs. Mellins with news of our new little neighbor.

ANN ELIZA opens door and admits MRS MELLINS.

ANN ELIZA: Good evening, Mrs. Mellins.

MRS MELLINS: And to you, sisters. I'm happy to report both mother and infant doing well. Between us, I don't know how long her milk will last though—after all she's almost 35, which in my book is a little old to be nursing.

EVELINA: Our mother was older 'n that when I was born. She nursed me all right, ain't that so, Ann Eliza?

ANN ELIZA: She was 40, that's right....and she didn't have no trouble with her milk. No trouble at all.

EVELINA: No, the trouble started later.

MRS MELLINS: What was that?

ANN ELIZA: You would mean the cancer.

EVELINA: Yes. What killed her when I was—how old was I, Ann Eliza?

ANN ELIZA: You was just four years old.

EVELINA: For a long time, I thought Ann Eliza was my real mother.

MRS MELLINS: Well, you couldn't a had a better one.

ANN ELIZA: Would you like a cup of tea, Mrs. Mellins? I was just making some.

ANN ELIZA moves back into the living area.

MRS MELLINS: (*following her*) Why that would be lovely—and then Evelina can tell me all about her visit to— (*spotting the clock on the shelf*) Oh, there she is! Must have been a success.

ANN ELIZA: (*pouring the tea*) Oh, more than that—seems Mr. Ramy practically told Evelina his whole life's story.

MRS MELLINS: Oh! How exciting!

EVELINA: Yes, he's a very important man. He was at Tiff'ny's before he started his own business.

MRS MELLINS: His own business! Oh, my.

EVELINA: He don't look rich though. His clothes are a little threadbare.

MRS MELLINS: Well, you and your sister can help fix that.

EVELINA: Yes, a little mending and patching here and there.

ANN ELIZA: You two are acting like a couple of school girls—trying to dress up Mr. Ramy like he was some kinda toy doll.

EVELINA: And guess what! He's coming by here day after tomorrow.

MRS MELLINS: Really? You invited him?

EVELINA: No. He—well he sorta invited hisself. So he could check up on the clock.

ANN ELIZA: Yes, isn't that nice, Mrs Mellins? Perhaps he can tell you the rest of his life story, Evelina.

The doorbell clangs.

ANN ELIZA: Now who could that be?

MRS MELLINS: Probably one of the Hawkins kids. I hope little Sheila's okay.

ANN ELIZA goes into the shop to the front door. There is the sound of muffled voices...."Well, hello"...."I hope I'm not disturbing you."..."why, no, not at all. Come in"...and we see ANN ELIZA escorting MR HERMAN RAMY into the shop and on into the living quarters. He is a tall gaunt man with a pale complexion; he wears a threadbare overcoat.

ANN ELIZA: Everyone, this is Mr. Ramy. I believe you already made the acquaintance of my sister (*indicates*

EVELINA). And this is our upstairs neighbor Mrs. Mellins.

MRS MELLINS: My pleasure, sir, I'm sure.

EVELINA: (*moving into the shop area*) May I assist you with your coat, Mr Ramy?

RAMY: Thank you, Miss Bunner.

EVELINA helps MR RAMY off with his coat and hangs it on the coat rack. She then picks up a small artificial flower from the work table, which she surreptitiously puts in her hair. She also rubs her cheeks to redden them. None of this goes unnoticed by ANN ELIZA.

RAMY: I hope I ain't bothering you ladies. I was on my way home from the shop and I found myself on your street— Miss Evelina give me your address.

ANN ELIZA shoots EVELINA a look of disapproval.

RAMY: (*continuing*) ...I saw the light on back here, so I thought I'd check up on the baby.

MRS MELLINS: (*confused*) Oh? Do you know the Hawkins?

ANN ELIZA: No, no—he ain't talking about little Sheila.

RAMY: Sheila? I don't know no Sheila. No, I'm talking about...(*scouring the room, until he sees the clock on the shelf*) that there clock back there! I don't like to led any clocks go out of my store without being sure it gives satisfaction.

EVELINA: Oh, *our* baby! She went beautiful ever since you fixed her.

MR RAMY goes to the clock and listens to it carefully.

RAMY: Well, ladies...(*a beat while he keeps them in suspense*) that clock's all right. I don't think you'll have anything to worry about from now on.

ANN ELIZA: That's good news. But won't you suit yourself to a seat?

RAMY: I don't want to bother you.

ANN ELIZA: We was just finishing up. Would you like some tea?

EVELINA: Or, perhaps--?

She glances at ANN ELIZA and then at the cupboard in the hutch.

ANN ELIZA: Yes, my sister's suggesting you have some cordial.

RAMY: Schnapps?

ANN ELIZA opens the cupboard door and brings out a bottle of cherry brandy. MR RAMY sits at the table.

ANN ELIZA: It's a cold night, Mr. Ramy. A sip of this'd do ya good. It was made a long time ago by our grandmother. We had 12 bottles once—now we only got a few left.

MRS MELLINS: You should be honored, Mr Ramy. The Bunner sisters only bring out their cherry cordial when somebody's sick—or for special guests and special occasions.

ANN ELIZA: This is to thank Mr. Ramy for fixing our baby.

She pours four glasses of cordial—the largest for MR RAMY.

RAMY: But you give too much to me—you don't take enough for yourselves.

ANN ELIZA: That's all right. My sister and I seldom partake

in spirits.

MRS MELLINS: Actually, I wouldn't say no to a wee bit more.

ANN ELIZA pours a little more into her glass.

MRS MELLINS: Thank you, Miss Bunner.

RAMY: (*holding his glass up to the light*) It looks real fine. To your baby!

The ladies raise their glasses in a toast.

EVELINA: Yes! Yes! To our baby!

They all drink.

MRS MELLINS: I hear you worked for Tiff'ny's, Mr. Ramy. You must a rubbed shoulders with all sorts of fancy people up there on Fifth Avenue.

RAMY: Not really, madam. Them rich people usually sends the housekeeper to bring things in and pick 'em up.

EVELINA has now picked up a half-finished artificial flower and starts working on it.

RAMY: You make flowers, I see, ma'am.

EVELINA: Ah well, yes, I do.

RAMY: It's a very pretty work. I had a lady friend in Germany that used to make flowers.

EVELINA: (*her smile diminished*) Oh.

MRS MELLINS: You left Germany a long time ago, Mr. Ramy?

RAMY: Dear me, yes. I was still in my twenties.

MRS MELLINS: Why did you come over?

RAMY: I was working for a clockmaker in Dusseldorf. He was a good man, but he paid me almost nuttin'. I could see there was no future with him and not much future in Germany neither. But I had a cousin lived in St. Louis. He was working in a brewery, making good money. He said he could get me a job there too— and I could stay with him. So I went, but I didn't like it. Too hot in summer, too cold in winter, and too many Germans. And all day the smell of beer...in the air, in your clothes, everywhere.

MRS MELLINS: How did you come to New York?

RAMY: I had a letter from the man I worked for in Dusseldorf. He told me about this wonderful store—jewelry, crystal, stained glass, watches, clocks. On Fifth Avenue in New York. He said if I could ever work there, it would be a paradise. So when I had enough money to leave St. Louis, I came here and I took my letter to Tiff'ny's and they give me a job.

MRS MELLINS: So why did you leave this paradise?

RAMY: Well, I took sick. Real sick. So I had to leave. And when I got better, I thought maybe it was time to go into business for myself. So I found the shop off Stuyvesant Square. But I am talking too much. I am boring you, I think.

EVELINA: Oh, no, Mr. Ramy. Not at all.

MRS MELLINS: We don't get many gentlemen visitors here.

RAMY: Still, I think I should be going. (*standing, to MRS MELLINS*) It was a pleasure to meet you, Madam...(*to ANN ELIZA and EVELINA*) and to see you again, ladies.

ANN ELIZA: It is our pleasure. Perhaps you will come again—for dinner the next time.

MR RAMY moves into the shop area where ANN ELIZA helps him on with his coat.

RAMY: Why, thank you. That would be real nice. (*looking at the room*) You're pleasantly fixed here; it looks real cozy.

EVELINA: Oh, we live very plainly. We have very simple tastes.

RAMY: You look real comfortable. I wish I had as good a store—but I guess no place seems homelike when you're alone in it.

ANN ELIZA: You are welcome to feel at home here whenever you like.

EVELINA: And you can check up on our baby!

He looks at the clock and then notices the ornate porcelain figurine of the woman next to it.

RAMY: And such a beautiful companion for the baby! Dresden porcelain, if I'm not mistaken.

ANN ELIZA: It also belonged to our grandmother. She come over in 1848—during the revolutions. She brought it on the boat with her and somehow it never got broke—and they had terrible storms.

EVELINA: It's Marie Antoinette. She was a French queen.

ANN ELIZA: I'm sure Mr. Ramy knows who Marie Antoinette was.

MRS MELLINS: And how she ended up (*indicates a slicing gesture across her neck with her hand*)...chop!

EVELINA: Well, our Marie Antoinette ain't gonna end up that way.

RAMY: (*carefully picking up the figurine to examine it*) Well, that's good, because she's very valuable. You know that?

ANN ELIZA: I never had her appraised. I would never part with her anyway—she means a lot to us. We have so little family—so few connections with the old country.

RAMY: Take good care of her—especially when you're dusting.

EVELINA: Don't worry; we do.

RAMY: Well, good-night, ladies. Thank you again for your hospitality—and for the cordial.

ANN ELIZA: (*handing MR RAMY his coat*) You're most welcome, Mr. Ramy.

EVELINA: Most welcome indeed.

MRS MELLINS: *Auf Wiedersehen!*

RAMY: Ah, you speak German?

MRS MELLINS: *Ein bisschen Deutsch.* My second husband was from Vienna.

RAMY: Where is he now?

MRS MELLINS: Probably dead—or in jail.

RAMY: Oh, I am sorry.

MRS MELLINS: Don't be. He deserves both. You remember that big bank robbery in Chicago ten years ago—over a hundred thousand dollars? Well, he was the mastermind behind that. They wanted me to testify, but naturally--

ANN ELIZA: Don't start with that old story again, please, Mrs. Mellins. (*to RAMY*) Don't mind Mrs. Mellins. We never know if she's telling the truth or just repeating some story she read in the *Police Gazette.*

RAMY: Well, what do they say? Truth is stranger than fiction.

MRS MELLINS: That's what I always say, too. We understand each other, don't we, Mr. Ramy?

RAMY: Yes...well....I guess...

ANN ELIZA: (*saving him*) Good night, Mr. Ramy, it's been our pleasure.

EVELINA: Yes, good night, Mr. Ramy. (*holding out her hand*) Enchanté

RAMY: Now French! You are polyglot here.

EVELINA: What? What's that?

RAMY: It means speaking many languages.

EVELINA: Oh, what a charming word. Poly...glot.

ANN ELIZA: (*easing RAMY to the door*) So, Mr. Ramy, I hope we will see you again.

RAMY: I look forward to that.

ANN ELIZA: We, too. Good night, sir.

RAMY: Good night, ladies.

RAMY leaves and ANN ELIZA returns to the other two women. For a moment, they are speechless, as each takes in MR RAMY's visit in a different way.

MRS MELLINS: Well...he's certainly an intelligent man.

EVELINA: Yes. And so polite.

ANN ELIZA: I think it's time we put away the cordial.

MRS MELLINS: (*holding out her glass*) Might I have just a spot more?

ANN ELIZA: You've already had a big glass. You know we keep it just for special occasions.

Nonetheless, she pours a little more into MRS MELLINS' glass.

MRS MELLINS: Well, this is still sort of a special occasion.

ANN ELIZA: What do you mean?

MRS MELLINS: Your visitor. I could tell—he has an eye for someone here.

EVELINA: And who might that be, Mrs. Mellins?

MRS MELLINS: Why you, dearie, of course.

EVELINA: Oh, do you think so?

MRS MELLINS: I do. In fact, I predict there'll be a wedding here sooner than you think.

ANN ELIZA: Well, we know that Evelina is always the center of attention. But I think you've had a little too much cordial, Mrs. Mellins.

MRS MELLINS: No, I know about these things.

ANN ELIZA: Nonsense. Just because a man is polite don't mean he's about to propose marriage.

EVELINA: How would you know, sister? I mean no disrespect, but you've never had a man in your life.

ANN ELIZA: And what about you, little sister? You and that Sunday School teacher? The one that came to supper every evening for six months and never brought so much as a loaf of bread before he disappeared from the face of the earth.

EVELINA: Well, at least I had him for a while. You never had nobody.

ANN ELIZA: Well, I guess I didn't have much time for all that, did I—looking after you for almost 30 years, not to mention minding a shop.

MRS MELLINS: Oh, dear. It looks like I've started something. I think I'd better go up and see how little Sheila is doing.

ANN ELIZA: Yes, you do that, Mrs. Mellins. (*back in control*) And tell Mrs. Hawkins if she needs anything, I'll be happy to help her.

MRS MELLINS: (*exiting*) I will, Miss Bunner. And thank you for the cordial. (*stopping to pat the clock*) That there's the cause of all your squabbling.

EVELINA: Oh, I don't think so. It's just two sisters quarreling with one another from time to time.

MRS MELLINS: Anyway, thanks again for the drink (*winks at EVELINA*)...and don't worry, dearie, your Mr. Ramy will be round again.

MRS MELLINS exits. The sisters return to putting away the cordial glasses. After, a slightly awkward pause...

EVELINA: I'm sorry, sister, if I offended you.

34

ANN ELIZA: And I'm sorry too—bringing up your Sunday School teacher.

EVELINA: Oh, I've forgotten about him. But, sister, sometimes I just wish—

ANN ELIZA: What?

EVELINA: I mean, Ann Eliza...don't you ever get tired of doing everything in one room?

ANN ELIZA: I always thought we was so comfortable here. Just like Mr. Ramy noticed.

EVELINA: Well, we are...comfortable enough. But I don't suppose there's any harm in saying I wished we had a parlor, is there? And we might manage to buy a screen big enough to hide the bed.

ANN ELIZA: I always think if we ask for more, what we have may be taken from us.

EVELINA: (*with a laugh, as she sweeps up the tablecloth*) Well, nobody'd get much around here. Except for Marie Antoinette up there and our new baby, of course.

ANN ELIZA: (*taking off the spread of the bed they share)* I think it's time for bed.

EVELINA: But, sister, don't you ever dream...of something else...of something different?

ANN ELIZA: And what would that be?

EVELINA: Maybe someone to share—whatever we have—share it with?

ANN ELIZA: You have someone to share it with. You've had someone to share it with for almost 30 years.

EVELINA: Oh, I'm sorry, sister. I didn't mean it like that...I meant—

ANN ELIZA: If you'd like to move out, sister, you're welcome to—

EVELINA: No, I meant— well, I meant a husband. Didn't you ever feel that way?

ANN ELIZA: I'm past all that, sister.

EVELINA: But maybe I ain't. I...I wanna be married, sister. I wanna wear silk on Sundays, I wanna take a part in a Church circle, and maybe even have a baby. Before it's too late. Oh, Ann Eliza, do you think Mrs. Mellins was right? Do you think he found me pretty?

ANN ELIZA: Well, of course he did. You're a pretty girl. But you should hold your horses. You know as well as I that if you go too fast, you sometimes have to rip out the whole seam. Now get undressed and go to bed, and thank the Lord that we've got a roof over our heads, food to eat, and our shop where we're not beholden to nobody.

EVELINA: But didn't you ever...ever think about having a husband?

ANN ELIZA: I told you. I never had time for that. I promised our mother on her deathbed that I'd take care of you.

EVELINA: And I'm thankful for that.

ANN ELIZA: I don't want your thanks. I had no choice in the matter. We're the same flesh and blood.

EVELINA: But didn't you ever feel that way about someone—you know, when your heart skips a beat?

ANN ELIZA: (*in fact feeling something she's not felt before*) No....I....I mean, sister, that's enough about Mr. Ramy for one night. You're too young for him, anyway.

EVELINA: Do you really think he's 40?

ANN ELIZA: I would put him around that age.

EVELINA: That's your age. Maybe you should think about him for yourself. That would be funny, wouldn't it?

ANN ELIZA: What?

EVELINA: If you was to get married—at your age!

ANN ELIZA: I said enough of this silly talk. Nobody's getting married in this house at any age—no matter what Mrs. Mellins says. It ain't in our hands, anyway.

EVELINA: Maybe it is—just a little.

EVELINA goes behind the screen and starts undressing.

EVELINA: Do you think he'll come back...like he said?

ANN ELIZA: I don't know. We'll have to wait and see.

EVELINA: That's easy for you.

ANN ELIZA: (*enigmatically*) Maybe it ain't.

EVELINA: What do you mean?

ANN ELIZA: Oh, nuttin', sister. Go on now. Say your prayers and go to sleep.

The clock ticks softly as ANN ELIZA turns down the bed. The sound of the clock crescendos, as the lights fade to black.

CURTAIN

ACT II

SCENE 1

Three months later; early spring. We hear the sound of a carrousel calliope playing a waltz. The music fades and the lights come up to reveal ANN ELIZA, EVELINA, and MRS MELLINS sitting around the kitchen table, enraptured by MR RAMY, who is standing in front of them reading Henry Wadsworth Longfellow's poem Maidenhood. *They are all drinking schnapps, which MR RAMY has brought.*

MR RAMY: MAIDEN! with the meek, brown eyes,
                  In whose orbs a shadow lies
                  Like the dusk in evening skies!

                  Thou whose locks outshine the sun,
                  Golden tresses, wreathed in one,
                  As the braided streamlets run!

                  Standing, with reluctant feet,
                  Where the brook and river meet,
                  Womanhood and childhood fleet!

                  Gazing, with a timid glance,
                  On the brooklets swift advance,
                  On the river's broad expanse!

Deep and still, that gliding stream
Beautiful to thee must seem,
As the river of a dream.

Then why pause with indecision,
When bright angels in thy vision
Beckon thee to fields Elysian?

Oh, thou child of many prayers!
Life hath quicksands. Life hath snares!
Care and age come unawares!

Like the swell of some sweet tune
Morning rises into noon,
May glides onward into June.

Gather, then, each flower that grows,
When the young heart overflows,
To embalm that tent of snows.

Bear through sorrow, wrong, and ruth
In thy heart the dew of youth,
On thy lips the smile of truth.

And that smile, like sunshine, dart
Into many a sunless heart,
For a smile of God thou art.

The ladies clap gently.

EVELINA: Oh, Mr. Ramy. What a beautiful poem.

MRS MELLINS: And you read it so well. You should have been an actor, Mr. Ramy.

RAMY: Ah, no...but I'm glad you liked it. It's one of my favorites. (*sits*) I think Longfellow is your best poet. (*to Ann Eliza*) Did you like it, Miss Bunner?

ANN ELIZA: Very much. But it's sad.

EVELINA: What are you saying? It's beautiful—all about

gathering flowers and a young woman's sunshine smiles.

ANN ELIZA: But it's also about the maiden becoming a woman and how life has quicksands and snares.

MRS MELLINS: And "Care and age come unawares." He's right about that. Why it seems it was just yesterday that I had five suitors—all wanting to marry me. And I picked the wrong one, of course. And that was just the first!

ANN ELIZA: What do you think, Mr. Ramy?

RAMY: About the poem?

ANN ELIZA: Yes.

RAMY: I think it means different things to all of us—that's the beauty of poetry. But for me, the maiden is afraid of something. "Why pause with indecision, when angels beckon thee to fields Elysian?" Afraid of life...afraid of becoming a woman?

EVELINA: Oh? Do you think so?

RAMY: I do—but Mr. Longfellow tells her to be brave and she will triumph with her smile... "For a smile of God thou art."

EVELINA: Oh, good. I like happy endings.

RAMY: (*standing*) And now, I think I am boring you ladies enough. It's time I must be going.

ANN ELIZA: You ain't never boring us, Mr. Ramy. We've come to count on your visits.

MRS MELLINS: And your poems. But perhaps sometime you'll read something by Edgar Allen Poe. *Annabelle Lee*, where the lover sleeps in his dead sweetheart's crypt.

EVELINA: No, please. Something more romantic.

MRS MELLINS: What could be more romantic than a lover who never gives up—all the way to the grave?

RAMY: Well, perhaps. But before I leave, I have a different proposition for you ladies. Since it's been such a long winter and since it is almost spring, maybe next Sunday we make a little excursion? Spend the day in Central Park? The forsythia is close to blooming.

EVELINA: And the jonquils! (*indicating the flowers on the table*) I bought these just this morning.

RAMY: Very beautiful, Miss Bunner.

ANN ELIZA: If it's not too cold. Yes, that would be fine.

RAMY: You will come, also, Mrs. Mellins?

MRS MELLINS: I would, but Sundays I visit my daughter in Hoboken and them fat screaming creatures that, I'm sorry to say, are my grandchildren. Believe me, I'd rather spend the day with you, but she would murder me if I didn't show up. I just hope her drunken husband ain't there, too.

ANN ELIZA: Mrs. Mellins, please!

RAMY: (*a beat*) So, it will just be the three of us.

EVELINA: Yes, what a wonderful idea, Mr. Ramy. Thank you.

MR RAMY moves to the door in the shop area, where ANN ELIZA hands him his coat.

RAMY: Till next Sunday then.

ANN ELIZA and EVELINA: Yes. Till then.

RAMY: (*to ANN ELIZA*) Oh, before I go. I almost forgot. That financial business, Miss Bunner. The $200 you have at the Grand Central bank. I looked into the New York Trust Company and I think you will do much better putting your money there. You might want to think about it.

ANN ELIZA: Oh, yes.

RAMY: There's no urgency, of course.

ANN ELIZA: I understand and we appreciate your offer to help. Just let me know what I need to do.

RAMY: Of course, Miss Bunner. Perhaps next week. And now, goodbye, and thank you for the delicious dinner.

ANN ELIZA: And thank you for the schnapps.

RAMY: I'm afraid it don't hold a candle to your cordial—

MRS MELLINS: Oh, no, sir. It was very good.

RAMY: I'm glad you liked it.

ANN ELIZA helps him on with his coat.

RAMY: Thank you, Miss Bunner. And good-night, ladies.

Assorted smiles and "good nights" as ANN ELIZA lets MR RAMY out.

MRS MELLINS: Well, there's a real gentleman. Ain't many like him these days. (*to EVELINA*) And like that there poem says, "gather each flower that grows" now! Before "May glides into June" — and beyond, dearie!

ANN ELIZA: Don't start with your marriage talk again, Mrs. Mellins.

MRS MELLINS: All I'm saying is he's ripe for the picking. But he won't be much longer.

ANN ELIZA: Oh! Stop, please.

MRS MELLINS: And that visit to Central Park. I know what he's up to. He's gonna get you alone with him, Evelina. That's why he wanted me to come, too—so I could be with Ann Eliza when he disappears with you.

EVELINA: Oh, you really think so?

ANN ELIZA: She's talking nonsense again. (to MRS MELLINS) You are deliberately getting her all riled up.

EVELINA: You talk about me like I was some child. I'm almost 30 years old.

ANN ELIZA: I just don't want you to get hurt.

MRS MELLINS: No, you just don't want her to grow up.

ANN ELIZA: If you don't mind my saying so, Mrs. Mellins, our family is none of your business. This is a dangerous city, a dangerous world.

MRS MELLINS: Ah, yes. The quicksand and the snares. And you're afraid to get beyond them.

ANN ELIZA: And you?

MRS MELLINS: I've taken my chances.

ANN ELIZA: And look where that's gotten you. A string of ex-husbands—and all those horrid children and fat grandchildren you can't stand.

MRS MELLINS: At least I've lived—and it ain't all been bad. My third husband, for example. Big Mike the fireman. Tall, handsome, ummm—he's the one I wish was still around.

EVELINA: What happened to him?

MRS MELLINS: The scoundrel—he went and died on me. Just like that. I won't tell you where—or how.

EVELINA: Oh, please. Tell us.

MRS MELLINS: Well, let's just say we was in the middle of something...

ANN ELIZA: That's really enough now. I think you've had more than enough of Mr. Ramy's schnapps.

MRS MELLINS: And I wouldn't say no to a wee bit more.

ANN ELIZA: (*reluctantly filling her glass*) There, and then I think it's time we all said good-night.

MRS MELLINS: Umm....I'm gonna have sweet dreams tonight.

EVELINA: Of Big Mike?

MRS MELLINS: Maybe! And who are you gonna dream of, dearie?

ANN ELIZA: Good-night, Mrs. Mellins.

MRS MELLINS: Good-night, ladies.

She gives a wink to Evelina and leaves.

ANN ELIZA: That woman! I shouldn't let her get me so riled up.

EVELINA: She don't mean no harm.

ANN ELIZA: Yes, she does—she's a busy-body and the drink brings out the worst in her.

EVELINA: Well, she's Irish, after all.

ANN ELIZA: And all those stories of her husbands and her children—I don't believe the half of them.

EVELINA: Well, she does have a daughter in Hoboken— and she goes out there almost every Sunday.

ANN ELIZA: God only knows who she sees out there. Could be a man for all we know.

EVELINA: Now, you're sounding as bad as her.

ANN ELIZA: The drink brings out the worst in her and she brings out the worst in me.

EVELINA: Do you think she's right?

ANN ELIZA: About what?

EVELINA: Central Park.

ANN ELIZA: Please, Evelina. Stop thinking about him all the time.

EVELINA: But it's true. He's never asked us to go out with him before—except for that stereopticon exhibit at Chickering Hall.

ANN ELIZA: And then he took that turn and couldn't go.

EVELINA: He takes a lot of them turns.

ANN ELIZA: He don't eat enough. I think that's one of the reasons he visits us so often.

EVELINA: I hope that's not the only reason. Ann Eliza, I know he was looking at me in a special way tonight when he was reading his poem.

ANN ELIZA: If you think so. But we've got to be careful. We don't want to scare him off.

EVELINA: We?

ANN ELIZA: I mean you, of course.

EVELINA: But, like our dear Mrs. Mellins says, the clock

keeps ticking.

ANN ELIZA: Yes, it does—and right now it says it's almost eleven o'clock. (*taking bible from the hutch*) Time to say our prayers and go to bed.

EVELINA suddenly laughs.

ANN ELIZA: What's so funny, sister?

EVELINA: I'm just thinking about little Mrs. Mellins and her fireman—

ANN ELIZA: Well just get those thoughts out of your head—especially as you are about to talk to the Lord.

EVELINA: (*still laughing*) I know—but the idea of her, of her and her big fireman together, and then him dying....Can you just imagine!

ANN ELIZA starts laughing as well.

EVELINA: And why are you laughing, sister?

ANN ELIZA: That woman! She's got the devil in her. I'm sorry. I just lost control of myself. It's her. (*still laughing, she gives Evelina a hug*) Oh, sister, I do love you. My little maiden. And just remember, no matter what happens, we still got each other.

EVELINA: And I love you, sister. But—

ANN ELIZA: No "but's" tonight. And no dreams. Let's just go to sleep.

EVELINA: Good night, sister.

ANN ELIZA: Good night, sister.

EVELINA moves behind the screen to undress, while ANN ELIZA sits at the table with her bible. She breaks out in laughter one more time as the clock ticks loudly, then fades along with the lights.

SCENE 2

The following Sunday; about noon. ANN ELIZA is helping EVELINA on with the jacket of a rose-colored suit with puffed sleeves.

ANN ELIZA: You'll be the most fashionable woman in Central Park, sister.

EVELINA: I just hope we don't run into Mrs. Goldfarb. She won't like that we copied her sleeves.

ANN ELIZA: I'm sure she'd be flattered. Anyway, her crowd don't go to Central Park on weekends—more likely out to Bayside or up to the Catskills.

EVELINA: What are you wearing, sister?

ANN ELIZA: I'm...well, you know, I don't think I'm gonna go.

EVELINA: What? Why?

ANN ELIZA: You know, my throat's been bothering me ever since last night—and it ain't getting any better.

EVELINA: (*not devastated by this news*) Oh...sorry, sister. What do you think it is?

ANN ELIZA: Probably nuttin'—just a spring cold.

EVELINA: Well, I'm sure Mr. Ramy's gonna be disappointed.

The doorbell clangs.

EVELINA: (*excited*) Oh, that must be him.

ANN ELIZA: Now, calm down. I'll get it. You finish fixing your hair.

ANN ELIZA goes to the door and opens it, admitting MR RAMY.

ANN ELIZA: Good day, sir.

RAMY: And such a beautiful day, too, Miss Bunner, for a walk in the Park.

ANN ELIZA: I'm sure. But sadly, sir, I won't be joining you.

RAMY: Oh? Why not? I was looking forward to you coming.

ANN ELIZA: Just a little spring cold, I'm afraid.

RAMY: I'm sorry to hear that. You must be careful not to take a turn. I was real ill a few weeks ago, as you know.

ANN ELIZA: Yes—and we're so happy you're recovered.

EVELINA appears, obviously pleased with her new dress.

RAMY: And who is this lovely lady?

EVELINA: Oh, it's just an old frock.

RAMY: Very stylish—such unusual sleeves.

EVELINA: They're the latest style—from Paris.

ANN ELIZA helps EVELINA on with her cape.

EVELINA: (*kissing her sister*) Thank you, sister. I so wish you was coming with us.

RAMY: And I, too.

ANN ELIZA: You'll both be fine. Such a beautiful afternoon.

RAMY: Good-bye, Miss Bunner. I hope you are feeling better soon.

ANN ELIZA: Thank you. I'm sure I will. Just a spring cold.

MR RAMY and EVELINA exit. ANN ELIZA watches them leave, then picks up a style magazine from the work table and takes it into the living quarters, where she lies down on the bed. As she begins to read, the clock ticks softly and the lights dim slowly. In the distance, the sound of a calliope playing a waltz can be heard over the clock, which eventually chimes "four." The music and the clock fade out as the lights come back up and we see ANN ELIZA asleep on the bed as EVELINA comes in the door alone. She calls for her sister as she takes off her cape, then walks over to the sitting room area, where she finds her.

EVELINA: Sister? Is you awake.

ANN ELIZA: (*stirring*) Oh, dear. Evelina. What time is it?

EVELINA: It's just past four. How long have you been sleeping?

ANN ELIZA: Ever since you and Mr. Ramy left.

EVELINA: Are you sure you're all right?

ANN ELIZA: I...I must a needed the sleep. But you're back early, ain't you?

EVELINA: Oh? A little...I guess.

ANN ELIZA: (*moving to the work table*) So tell me about your afternoon. I bet it was wonderful?

EVELINA: Oh, sister, it was. The forsythia was all in bloom

and there was jonquils everywhere. We took the streetcar up
Madison Avenue; it was real crowded, but we found seats
around 34th Street, which was good because Mr. Ramy was
still kinda weak it seemed.

ANN ELIZA: Yes, I thought he looked kinda pale.

EVELINA: Once we got to the park, he seemed to perk up.
We walked to the carrousel—it was so beautiful and I loved
the calliope music. Some tunes was waltzes. Mr. Ramy said
they was written by Strauss. He knows so much. Then we went
to the lake—all crowded with people in rowboats. He offered
to take me out in one of 'em—but there was a big line, so
instead we had an ice cream at the boathouse. I took off my
cape and I could tell people was looking at me—at the dress. I
think he was real proud to be with me.

ANN ELIZA: I'm sure he was. And after the boathouse?

EVELINA: Well, we was walking towards The Ramble, and
then something kinda funny happened.

ANN ELIZA: What was that?

EVELINA: We was crossing over that bridge—the one that
sorta bows up in the middle like what they have in Japan or
China. Anyway, we was walking over it and outta nowhere we
heard someone calling "Ramy…hey Ramy." Mr. Ramy turned
around and we could see this rough-looking man coming
towards us. I was kinda scared, to tell you the truth. The man
seemed real angry and he was talking German. Mr. Ramy was
real upset. He asked me to wait at one end of the bridge while
he went and talked to him more or less in private. Eventually,
the man went back in the same direction he come from. Mr.
Ramy looked real pale by then. He told me the man was
someone he had worked with at Tiff'ny's and that he was
angry about something that happened at work a couple of
years ago. Said it wasn't important. So we kept on walking and

everything was beautiful again. Mr. Ramy pointed out different kinds of trees and bushes. He knows so much about so many things. But he was still pale and he asked if I'd mind if we cut the visit short. I said, of course, I understood completely.

ANN ELIZA: I'm so sorry, Evelina.

EVELINA: Why? It was a beautiful afternoon. Except for that man. (*pause*) You know, Mr. Ramy kissed my hand when he said goodbye. He ain't never done that before. Oh, and he mentioned your $200 again. Said I should remind you about letting him put it into another bank like you and he was talking about the other evening.

ANN ELIZA: Of course. Next time I see him. We'll work it out.

EVELINA: I just hope he's all right. I hope he don't take another turn or anything like that.

ANN ELIZA: I'm sure he's fine. Probably just a spring cold— like mine.

EVELINA starts sobbing gently.

ANN ELIZA: What's the matter, sister?

EVELINA: I hate that man! He ruined everything.

ANN ELIZA: Now, now.

EVELINA: I can't help thinking that Mr. Ramy had more to say to me...especially when we was walking over to The Ramble. It's such a romantic place. And then that horrid man came and—

ANN ELIZA: It's all right, sister. Everything will be all right. In due time. There will be more trips to the park. We just mustn't rush things.

EVELINA: You always say that.

ANN ELIZA: I know I do. But you know as well as I that if you go too fast...

EVELINA: Yes, yes, I know—you have to rip out the whole seam! You know, sometimes I think you don't want him to propose to me.

ANN ELIZA: Now why on earth would you think that?

EVELINA: I think you like everything just the way it is—with him coming around for dinner and playing cards and reading his poetry...

ANN ELIZA: And you don't enjoy his visits?

EVELINA: I do, but I want more.

ANN ELIZA: And I keep telling you to be patient.

EVELINA: And I don't know how much longer I can.

ANN ELIZA: There, there—I'll make us some tea. You'll feel better after a nice cup. And I have the pound cake you like here, too, from Mrs. Hawkins. Don't cry. Everything will be all right.

The clock ticks softly and the calliope waltz comes up again as the lights go down.

SCENE 3

The following Saturday; around 2:00 in the afternoon. ANN ELIZA is alone in the shop, sorting buttons from a basket on the worktable. The door opens slowly; the bell hasn't rung.

ANN ELIZA looks around to see MR RAMY entering.

ANN ELIZA: Why Mr. Ramy, what a surprise. Is something wrong?

RAMY: Not's I know of. I always close up the store for an hour at 2 o'clock Saturdays at this season, so I thought I might as well call round and see you.

ANN ELIZA: I'm real glad, I'm sure, but you just missed Evelina.

RAMY: I know that. I met her over in the Square. She was getting on the streetcar to go to your new dyer's up in 48th Street. She'll be gone for a bit I guess.

ANN ELIZA: (*confused*) Yes, I imagine so. (*indicating stool alongside worktable*) Won't you set down?

RAMY: (*sitting*) Well, I guess we're very well here.

Seeing MR RAMY looking at her with unusual intensity, ANN ELIZA pushes a few strands of hair off her temples, and straightens the brooch beneath her collar.

ANN ELIZA: Would you perhaps like a cup of tea?

RAMY: That would be nice—but I don't have so much time. (*pause, indicates for her to sit as he continues to gaze at her*) You're looking very well today, Miss Bunner. I guess you are over your cold.

ANN ELIZA: Oh, it didn't amount to much.

RAMY: I guess you're healthier than your sister, even if you are less sizeable.

ANN ELIZA: Oh, I don't know. Evelina's a mite nervous sometimes, but she ain't a bit sickly.

RAMY: She eats healthier than you do, but that don't mean nuttin'.

Silence. ANN ELIZA does not follow the point of this conversation.

RAMY: Well, Miss Bunner (*drawing stool closer to counter*), I guess I might as well tell you what I come here for today.

ANN ELIZA: Please do.

RAMY: I want to get married.

ANN ELIZA: Well, uh, Mr. Ramy, I thought sooner or later you'd be—mercy me, Mr. Ramy!

RAMY: I want to get married. I'm too lonesome. It ain't good for a man to live all alone and eat nuttin' but cold meat every day.

ANN ELIZA: (*softly*) No.

RAMY: And the dust fairly beats me.

ANN ELIZA: The dust—I know.

RAMY: (*stretching his hand awkwardly towards her and taking her hand in his*) I wish you'd take me.

ANN ELIZA: Me—me?

RAMY: I guess so. You suit me right down to the ground, Miss Bunner. That's the truth.

ANN ELIZA is shocked, silent.

RAMY: (*withdrawing his hand*) Maybe you don't fancy me?

ANN ELIZA: I don't say that.

RAMY: Well, I always kinder thought we was suited to one another. I always liked the quiet style—no fuss and no airs, and not afraid of work.

ANN ELIZA: But Mr. Ramy, you don't understand. I never thought of marrying.

RAMY: Why not?

ANN ELIZA: Well, I don't know, har'ly. The fact is, I ain't as active as I look. Maybe I couldn't stand the care. I ain't as spry as Evelina—nor as young.

RAMY: But you do most of the work here. You run things, take care of the orders, and the finances. I want a woman—not a child.

ANN ELIZA: But Evelina's almost 30; she's not a child.

RAMY: Oh, I know. It's just her way of behaving—you know, so excited all the time. Not serious like you.

ANN ELIZA: I don't think you know her well enough. She works hard. She's busy on the outside. I'm the oldest. I have to look after things here.

RAMY: (*taking her hand* again) I could help you do that.

ANN ELIZA: No, no. I couldn't, Mr. Ramy. I'm just so surprised. I always thought it was Evelina—always. And so did everybody else. She's so bright and pretty—it seemed so natural.

RAMY: Well, you was all mistaken.

ANN ELIZA: I'm so sorry.

RAMY: (*rising*) You better would think it over.

ANN ELIZA: No, no—it ain't any sorter use, Mr. Ramy. I

don't never mean to marry. I get tired so easy—and I have such awful headaches.

RAMY: Headaches, do you? You never—

ANN ELIZA: My, yes, awful ones, that I have to give right up to. Evelina has to do everything when I have one of them darned things.

RAMY: Well, I'm sorry to hear it.

ANN ELIZA: Thank you kindly all the same, and please don't...don't tell—

RAMY: Oh, that's all right. Don't you fret, Miss Bunner. Folks gotta suit themselves.

An awkward pause...

RAMY: I don't want this should make any difference between us.

ANN ELIZA: Oh my, no. You'll come by just the same. We'd miss you awfully if you didn't. Evelina, she—

RAMY: Don't Miss Evelina have no headaches?

ANN ELIZA: My, no, never—well, not to speak of, anyway. She ain't had one for ages, and when Evelina is sick, she won't never give in to it.

RAMY: I wouldn't a thought that.

ANN ELIZA: I guess you don't know us as well as you thought you did.

RAMY: Well, no, that's so, maybe I don't. So, I guess I better be going.

ANN ELIZA: Are you sure you won't have a cup of tea?

RAMY: Thank you, madam. I gotta get back to the shop.

ANN ELIZA: Oh, I see. Well, thank you for the visit.

RAMY: And maybe you'll think just a little bit more about what I said. I mean, you're sure, ya?

ANN ELIZA: Oh, Mr. Ramy. I just couldn't. I mean, my whole life—it's been for Evelina. I couldn't leave her—I just couldn't do this to her.

RAMY: You don't have to leave her. She's still your sister.

ANN ELIZA: You don't understand.

RAMY: As you wish, then. So...good-day, Miss Bunner.

ANN ELIZA: Good-day, Mr. Ramy. And we agree—we won't talk about this to Evelina.

RAMY: Of course not. I am a man of my word.

With a slight bow, he is out the door. After he leaves, ANN ELIZA finds herself in a dreamy state. At first she just stands by the door, watching RAMY disappear. Then she moves to the mirror and looks at herself, again pulling her hair back. Perhaps for the first time in her life, she is satisfied with the way she looks. Smiling, she walks to the table where RAMY has proposed to her. She faces his stool and closes her eyes as she savors the proposal in her mind. But when she opens her eyes and sees only the empty shop, she starts to cry. She quickly blots her tears when she realizes that EVELINA has returned.

EVELINA: (*setting a large bundle on the worktable*) My goodness, sister, what in heaven is the matter?

ANN ELIZA: Oh, nuttin'. Just some dust in my eye.

EVELINA: Here, let me take a look at it.

ANN ELIZA: No, I'm fine, sister.

EVELINA: Guess who I seen at the streetcar earlier?

ANN ELIZA: Who?

EVELINA: Our Mr. Ramy.

ANN ELIZA: Yes, he was just here.

EVELINA: He was? He didn't tell me he was coming by when I saw him. He knew I wasn't gonna be here.

ANN ELIZA: Can't he want to see me, too?

EVELINA: Yes—but why, I wonder. He didn't ask you anything, did he? Anything important?

Ann Eliza looks confused.

EVELINA: You see, I started thinking on the streetcar—about Central Park and that terrible man 'n all. And it dawned on me that maybe if Mr. Ramy's gonna ask me something important—maybe he thinks he should talk to you first—'cuz you're so much older than me 'n all. I think sometimes he's thinking of you like you was my mother, so if he wanted to do something special, well—

ANN ELIZA: What?

EVELINA: I mean, if he wanted to ask me to marry him, well, he's old-fashioned and maybe he's thinking he needs to ask you first—for your permission.

ANN ELIZA: Maybe he does, but that ain't why he stopped by. It may be hard for you to believe, sister, but maybe he just wanted to see me. For a friendly visit.

EVELINA: But he sees you whenever he comes over for dinner. I just don't understand why he'd want to see you alone—unless he had a reason.

ANN ELIZA: (*a beat*) Actually he came here to—

EVELINA: What?

ANN ELIZA: Well, did you ever think, sister, that maybe the world doesn't only just revolve around you?

EVELINA: What do you mean? What's the matter with you, sister? You ain't making any sense. He must a upset you. What did he say?

ANN ELIZA: (*after a pause*) He asked me to— No, no, I can't—

EVELINA: What? What is it?

ANN ELIZA: I mean you was sorta right; he didn't want my permission to let you marry him, but he wanted to know how you felt about it. I said I'd ask you. Now we don't want him to think you're too anxious.

EVELINA: But I am.

ANN ELIZA: But he moves slow, our Mr. Ramy. We don't want to frighten him. You gotta give him a little time.

EVELINA: Oh, I'll give him all the time in the world. But I can't stand it much longer.

ANN ELIZA: I'll talk to him then.

EVELINA: Would you? Oh, it would be so wonderful, sister. I mean if it don't happen soon, I might as well resign myself to being an old maid— I'm sorry, Ann Eliza. I didn't mean—

ANN ELIZA: Never mind, Evelina. Some of us is cut out to be

married and some of us— (*smiles enigmatically*) well...not being married ain't the end of the world.

EVELINA: (*not hearing her*) Oh, sister, I'm so happy. (*hugging her*) Thank you, Ann Eliza. Thank you.

The calliope waltz comes up again, but it now sounds decidedly discordant, as the lights fade.

SCENE 4

About a month later; a sunny Sunday in early June. MRS MELLINS is standing at the door drinking a glass of lemonade while ANN ELIZA cuts fabric for what appears to be an especially tiny dress. She holds it up for MRS MELLINS to see.

MRS MELLINS: What are you doing, Miss Bunner—making costumes for Ringling Brothers now?

ANN ELIZA: This ain't for no circus dwarf, if that's what you're trying to say. It's for a little girl.

MRS MELLINS: What little girl?

ANN ELIZA: Mrs. Goldfarb's granddaughter.

MRS MELLINS: Granddaughter! She's too young to have grandchildren, ain't she?

ANN ELIZA: Would you believe—she's almost 50.

MRS MELLINS: Maybe she had one of them there new-fangled operations—like what I read about they're doing in France and Berlin. They cut the skin outta the side of your head and then tie it back behind your ears and stitch it all up. A face-lift, they call it. But if they don't do it right, you end up looking like a Frankenstein monster.

ANN ELIZA: Oh, don't be silly, Mrs. Mellins. She's just taken good care of herself.

MRS MELLINS: Well I guess so—all that money and not having to work can do wonders.

ANN ELIZA: She does work though—at some charity for them poor people come over from Russia down on the Lower East Side.

MRS MELLINS: Jews.

ANN ELIZA: I believe so.

MRS MELLINS: So she helps raise 'em up, so then they can move into one of her father's over-priced tenements on Delancy.

ANN ELIZA: Stop, please! You know I don't like that kinda talk.

The clock chimes.

MRS MELLINS: Five o'clock. The "couple" is out later than usual.

ANN ELIZA: That's 'cuz they didn't go to the Park today.

MRS MELLINS: Oh? Where did they go?

ANN ELIZA: Evelina felt like a little ocean air, so they went for a sail in Jamaica Bay on one of them Coney Island boats.

MRS MELLINS: Still no proposal?

ANN ELIZA: No.

MRS MELLINS: But Evelina keeps hoping?

ANN ELIZA: I guess she does, yes.

MRS MELLINS: But what about you? If they ever do get married, and I have no doubts they will, you're gonna be awful lonely here without your little sister around.

ANN ELIZA: She'll still be coming round to help me with the shop.

MRS MELLINS: Oh, she says that now—but just wait. Especially once they have a couple of brats—you won't see her near as much, unless she wants you to mind her little hellions. You don't know about these things, being cooped up in this shop all these years.

ANN ELIZA: I know more about "things" than you think, Mrs. Mellins—and I'm sick and tired of the way you and Evelina make me out to be some ignorant old maid. It's the two of you that are the ignorant ones. Evelina with her fairy-tale notions that a knight on horseback's gonna swoop down and change her life. And you with your magazines and crazy stories. You two don't have to explain nuttin' to me. I can take care of myself. I spent my whole life doing that.

MRS MELLINS: No…you spent your whole life taking care of Evelina.

There is the sound of people outside the door to the shop. It's RAMY and EVELINA.

ANN ELIZA: Shhh! They're back. I don't want Mr. Ramy hearing us going on like this.

EVELINA comes into the shop and RAMY walks off.

MRS MELLINS: Well, my dear, I hear you've been out sailing.

EVELINA: (*taking off her spring coat and bonnet*) Oh we

was. It was lovely.

MRS MELLINS: And where's Mr. Ramy?

EVELINA: He was feeling tired—so he's gone back to his rooms.

MRS MELLINS: I worry about his health. He should eat better—needs someone to cook his dinners for him.

ANN ELIZA: He sure eats all right when he's here.

MRS MELLINS: But that's only every week or so. (*winking at EVELINA*) He needs someone every night. Which reminds me—the Hawkins have invited me up for supper tonight, so I'd best be going. Corned beef and cabbage—ugh! And that awful little Shelia will be screaming her head off through most of the meal. But beggars can't be choosers. Anyway, good day, Miss Bunner...Evelina.

MRS MELLINS exits, and ANN ELIZA goes back to working on MRS GOLDFARB'S grand-daughter's dress, as EVELINA hovers around the room anxiously.

EVELINA: Well—ain't you even got time to ask me if I had a pleasant day?

ANN ELIZA: I guess I don't have to. Seems to me it's pretty plain.

EVELINA: Well, I don't know. I don't know how I feel—it's all so queer. I almost think I'd like to scream.

ANN ELIZA: I guess you're tired.

EVELINA: No, I ain't. It's not that. But it all happened so suddenly, and the boat was so crowded I thought everybody would hear what he was saying. —Ann Eliza, why on earth don't you ask me what I'm talking about?

ANN ELIZA: What *are* you?

EVELINA: Why, I'm engaged to be married—so there! Now it's out! Only to think of it! Of course I've known right along he was going to sooner or later—but somehow I didn't think of it happening today. I mean right on the boat. I thought he'd never get up the courage. Well, I ain't said yes *yet*—leastways I told him I'd have to think it over; but I guess he knows. And I ain't 30 yet, so I ain't gonna be a—

ANN ELIZA: No, Sister, you ain't...

EVELINA: Oh, Ann Eliza, I'm so happy.

ANN ELIZA: And I'm happy for you, little sister. (*moves to cabinet*) Here, let's get out the cordial.

EVELINA: Oh, yes. This is a real special occasion. (*looks at bed*) Just think, we won't be sleeping together in the same old bed anymore. You'll have it all to yourself.

ANN ELIZA: (*getting out cordial*) Why, yes. I'll have a lot of things to myself, won't I? But I'll get used to them. (*holding back tears*) Oh, I'm sorry , Evelina, I—

EVELINA: Don't cry, sister. This is a happy night.

ANN ELIZA: Of course it is. I'm crying because I'm so happy for you. Here, have some cordial. (*handing her a glass*) To Mrs. Herman Ramy.

EVELINA: It sounds nice, don't it?

ANN ELIZA: It does, Mrs. Ramy. My little maiden.

As they toast, the clock ticks, the lights fade.

SCENE 5

Six weeks later; early evening, mid-July. MRS MELLINS and ANN ELIZA are at the table, working on Evelina's wedding dress.

MRS MELLINS: But I thought he hated St. Louis.

ANN ELIZA: So did I. But he's gotta go where the work is.

MRS MELLINS: He seemed to be doing just fine here.

ANN ELIZA: I guess we was wrong about that—and now his landlord's doubled the rent on his little hole-in-the-wall.

MRS MELLINS: Oh, I know. It's getting so fancy over there around the Square. Pretty soon they won't let us common folk in there without showing our bankbooks.

ANN ELIZA: Anyway, his cousin found him an excellent position in the clock department of a big firm out there— the Tiff'n'ys of St. Louis, he says. It's a splendid opening and if he gives satisfaction, they'll raise him at the end of the year.

MRS MELLINS: What does Evelina think about all this?

ANN ELIZA: Don't ask her—'cuz she'll get all uppity. (*imitating EVELINA*) "You wouldn't have me interfere with his prospects, would you?"

MRS MELLINS: Oh, my!

ANN ELIZA: Still, I think she ain't so keen on the whole thing.

MRS MELLINS: Where's the love-birds now?

ANN ELIZA: Lately, they've taken to going to that there

new soda fountain over on Union Square—for egg creams, thank you very much!

Unbeknownst to the ladies, EVELINA has quietly entered the shop.

MRS MELLINS: (*with a start*) Mercy, Miss Evelina! I declare I thought you was a ghost, the way you crep' in.

EVELINA: I'm sorry, Mrs. Mellins. I didn't mean to startle you.

EVELINA sits downstage by the sewing machine; she seems exhausted.

MRS MELLINS: You do look dead beat. I guess Mr. Ramy lugs you round that Square too often. Where is Mr. Ramy, by the way—why ain't he honoring us with his presence?

EVELINA: I guess he don't always have to come in when he's dropped me off—

MRS MELLINS: Well, I guess not. I just woulda liked to see his face. I feel I ain't seen that much of him since—well, with the engagement and all. And now I hear you're going to St. Louis—

EVELINA: He ain't got that much time—with closing things down here and getting ready to leave. He barely has time to see me lately, so—

MRS MELLINS: Of course, dearie. I understand. Now, don't you want to take a good look at this dress we're slaving so hard on?

EVELINA: I'm kinda tired, Mrs. Mellins. I'm sure it's real beautiful—I'll look at it tomorrow.

ANN ELIZA: (*gathering up the pieces of the dress-in-*

progress) Maybe we'd better put away the work for tonight Mrs. Mellins. I guess what Evelina wants is a good night's rest.

MRS MELLINS: (*helping to put away the dress*) That's so. There, you go right away to bed, Miss Evelina; we'll set up again tomorrow night. Good-night, ladies.

ANN ELIZA: Thank you, Mrs Mellins.

MRS MELLINS exits and ANN ELIZA goes back to gathering up the wedding dress.

EVELINA: There ain't any use in going on with that.

ANN ELIZA: Evelina Bunner—what do you mean?

EVELINA: Just what I say. It's put off.

ANN ELIZA: Put off—what's put off?

EVELINA: Getting married. He can't take me to St. Louis. He ain't got money enough.

ANN ELIZA: I don't understand.

EVELINA: Well, it's plain enough. The journey's fearfully expensive and we've got to have something left to start with when we get out there. We've counted up, and he ain't got the money to do it, that's all.

ANN ELIZA: But I thought he was going right into a splendid place.

EVELINA: So he is, but the salary's pretty low the first year, and board's very high in St. Louis. He's just got another letter from his cousin out there, and he's been figuring it out, and he's afraid to chance it. He'll have to go alone.

ANN ELIZA: But there's your money—have you forgotten that? Your half of our two hundred in the bank.

EVELINA: Of course I ain't forgotten it. Only it ain't enough. It would all have to go into buying furniture, and if he took sick again and lost his place again, we wouldn't have a cent left. He says he's got to lay by another hundred dollars before he'll be willing to take me out there.

ANN ELIZA: Seems to me he might have thought of it before.

EVELINA: I guess he knows what's right as well as you or me. I'd sooner die than be a burden to him.

EVELINA goes into the living area, flops down on the bed in tears. ANN ELIZA follows her and sits beside her on the bed.

ANN ELIZA: Don't cry so, sister. Don't—

EVELINA: Oh, I can't bear it. I can't bear it.

ANN ELIZA: Don't, don't. If you take the other hundred, won't that be enough for the time being? I always meant to give it to you. Only I didn't want to tell you till your wedding day.

EVELINA: Oh, sister, do you think? I didn't want to beg— but, oh, I'd be so grateful.

ANN ELIZA: There, there. Go to sleep now. We have a big week ahead. You're gonna need all the rest you can get. It's not every day my little sister's getting married.

EVELINA: I never thought this day would come! I'm so happy. Thank you, sister.

ANN ELIZA: And I'm so happy for you...Mrs. Ramy. So happy.

The lights fade slowly. In the darkness, we hear a train whistle and the sound of a train speeding along the tracks. The train slows down and the sound fades out as the lights come up to reveal ANN ELIZA at the shop door with a letter. She opens it carefully and begins to read. The letter is from EVELINA, whose voice we hear over the scene.

EVELINA: (*Voice*) August 20, 1889...My Dearest Sister, I hope you will excuse the delay in writing to you but with the journey on the train and then the excitement of this new city, there just wasn't time to sit down and compose a proper epistle. I think often of the beautiful wedding in the chapel of our dear St. Mark's church and then the supper back at the shop with the handsome cake Mrs. Hawkins baked for the occasion.

It seems so strange to be in this great city so far from home, alone with him I have chosen for life. But marriage has its solemn duties, which those who are not married can never hope to understand. Not that I have cause to complain—my dear Husband is all love and devotion, but with him being alone all day at his business, how can I help but feel lonesome at times? I often wonder, my dear Sister, how you are getting along. May you never experience the feelings of solitude I have underwent since I came here, but had my lot been cast in a wilderness, I hope I should not repine, for they who exchange their independence for the sweet name of Wife must be prepared to find all is not gold that glitters.

Hoping this finds you as well as it leaves me, I remain, my Dear Sister, Yours Truly...Evelina B. Ramy

P.S. Another reason it's taken so long for me to write you, Dear Sister, is because of Marie Antoinette. I am so embarrassed. I didn't know she was to be traveling with us. He said he discussed it with you, but I am not so sure he did. He's sometimes real forgetful. But he promised me he's only pawning her, and as soon as he can get her out of hock, he will send her back to you right away. They pack clocks real good where he's working, and I'm sure they can do the same with ceramics. So she'll make the journey back to New York safe and sound.

Ann Eliza stands motionless; the clock ticks; the lights fade to black.

CURTAIN

ACT III

SCENE 1

The lights come up to reveal both the shop and the living quarters considerably less tidy than before. It is mid-morning, early February. Dirty dishes cover the dining table; in the shop, fabric and half-trimmed hats are strewn about. ANN ELIZA, wearing a housecoat, is at the worktable wrapping the clock in plain brown paper. The doorbell clangs. ANN ELIZA goes to the door and admits MRS MELLINS.

MRS MELLINS: Closed again? It's almost noon.

ANN ELIZA: It's also February—and freezing out there. Ain't no people that ain't crazy out shopping today. Anyway, with Evelina gone, I lost almost all my bonnet business. (*pause*) Nobody could trim a hat like my sister.

MRS MELLINS: I seen the postman was here this morning. I guess you still ain't heard nuttin'.

ANN ELIZA: No, and today makes it exactly three months. I did get another letter from Sergeant Schultz at the Police Department out there though. He thinks I should go myself to look for her. So, I've made a decision. If I ain't heard from her by the end of this month, I'm gonna follow his advice. He

70

promised to help me track her down.

MRS MELLINS: But what're you gonna do for money?

ANN ELIZA: I made another decision—(*indicates clock*) I'm pawnin' our baby.

MRS MELLINS: You're pawning everything, Miss Bunner, if you don't mind my saying so. Ain't gonna be nuthin' left here. I still don't know how you could stand to part with Marie Antoinette.

ANN ELIZA: I had to—I gave almost all our savings to the two of them to go to St. Louis. (*a beat*) I never shoulda let her marry him.

MRS MELLINS: What could you a done? She was in love with him.

ANN ELIZA: No—she was desperate. It coulda been anybody.

MRS MELLINS: But there wasn't anybody. There was just Ramy.

ANN ELIZA: I shoulda stopped it. I coulda.

MRS MELLINS: How could you a done that?

ANN ELIZA: There are things you don't know.

MRS MELLINS: What do you mean?

ANN ELIZA: He wasn't sure about Evelina. I—I convinced him, pushed him even—'cuz I knew how much she wanted, wanted not to wind up an old maid. And now it's over three months I ain't heard from her. I'm afraid she's lost...or sick...or ... Oh, god. My baby. (*breaks down*) And it's my fault. It's all my fault.

MRS MELLINS: Now, stop Ann Eliza. Stop blaming yourself.

ANN ELIZA: I gotta find her. I gotta save her—bring her back. I've wasted too much time already.

MRS MELLINS: You sure you done everything you can?

ANN ELIZA: Well, maybe not. I was thinking. If he looked for another job out there in St. Louis, he'd have to give references. And since he worked at Tiff'na'ys, he'd surely try to get references from them. And if he did, they'd have to have some kinda address to get back to him.

MRS MELLINS: So you need to go up to Tiff'na'ys then to find out.

ANN ELIZA: Yes, that's what I thought. But I realized I couldn't just go there.

MRS MELLINS: Why not?

ANN ELIZA: It's too fancy. They probably wouldn't even a let me in the door.

MRS MELLINS: Oh, that's crazy. This is America. They can't do that here.

ANN ELIZA: Oh yes they can. They don't even have to say nuttin' neither; they can just look at you a certain way and you'll turn right around and go the other direction. But I was thinking. Mrs. Goldfarb has me doing another one of them party dresses for her granddaughter. So I asked her last week when she was here if she would mind going and talking with someone in the clock department.

MRS MELLINS: And what did she say?

ANN ELIZA: She said she'd be happy to do it.

MRS MELLINS: Well, that's sure a surprise. I wouldn't think she'd want anything to do with our problems down here.

ANN ELIZA: You never give her proper credit. She's a good woman.

MRS MELLINS: Did she find out anything?

ANN ELIZA: She ain't found out nuttin' yet, far as I know. But she's dropping by this afternoon, so we'll see.

MRS MELLINS: Well, I don't like to tell people what to do, but if you have that rich Jewess coming by and she's done you a big favor, I'd straighten this place up some. It looks like a pigsty. I'll give you a hand.

ANN ELIZA: (*looking at the half-wrapped clock*) Oh, Lord, she'll be here any minute.

MRS MELLINS: So get out of that housecoat and get into something presentable. I'll straighten up the shop.

ANN ELIZA retreats to the living quarters and changes behind the screen. MRS MELLINS gathers up stray pieces of fabric and folds them neatly. She then arranges all the hats in a row on a display shelf. The doorbell clangs. She goes to the door and admits MRS GOLDFARB.

MRS MELLINS: Good day, Madam.

MRS GOLDFARB: Good day. I was expecting to find Miss Bunner.

MRS MELLINS: Yes, she's expecting you. Please come in. She'll be out in a moment. Can I get you a cup of tea?

MRS GOLDFARB: Oh, no, dear, thank you. I'm meeting some friends for lunch. It's very kind of you though.

ANN ELIZA, now dressed and coiffed to the best of her ability, enters.

ANN ELIZA: Ah, Mrs. Goldfarb. Please excuse me. I had a customer and got a bit behind. The dress is ready—you may want a few alterations though.

MRS GOLDFARB: I'm sure it's lovely. If it's half as nice as the last one, my granddaughter will be thrilled. Birthday party for one of the Loeb children. They're taking over Steeple-chase Park on Coney Island—she's a very excited little girl.

MRS MELLINS: Well, I'll leave you ladies to business.

ANN ELIZA: Yes, thank you, Mrs. Mellins. For your help.

MRS MELLINS: Any time, Miss Bunner. (*to MRS GOLDFARB*) Goodbye, madam.

MRS GOLDFARB: Goodbye.

MRS MELLINS exits. ANN ELIZA unfolds the little girl's party dress.

MRS GOLDFARB: Oh, yes! Even prettier than I expected.

ANN ELIZA: We could add a little piping here to the sleeves, if you like?

MRS GOLDFARB: Umm, I don't know. I think...well, maybe. It might be a nice touch.

ANN ELIZA: Of course, Mrs. Goldfarb. I could have it ready for you same time tomorrow..

MRS GOLDFARB: Perfect. (*a beat, as ANN ELIZA puts the dress away*) And now...I have some news for you. I stopped by Tiffany's yesterday.

ANN ELIZA: Oh?

MRS GOLDFARB: I saw a Mr. Loomis in the clock department.

ANN ELIZA: Yes? Did he know Mr. Ramy?

MRS GOLDFARB: Not at first, but after he looked through his records, he did find him.

ANN ELIZA: And?

MRS GOLDFARB: Miss Bunner, just how much do you know about your sister's husband?

ANN ELIZA: Not much, unfortunately. We know he was one of the heads of the clock department at Tiff'nay's—till he got sick.

MRS GOLDFARB: Well, it turns out he did work at Tiffany's, but he was not a department head. He was an ordinary worker, in the clock repair department.

ANN ELIZA: Oh.

MRS GOLDFARB: Not that there's anything wrong with that, of course. It's a good steady job.

ANN ELIZA: Of course.

MRS GOLDFARB: But do you know the circumstances of his leaving the company?

ANN ELIZA: Like I said, he got sick and by the time he got better, he decided to take a step up and start his own business with the shop on Stuyvesant Square.

MRS GOLDFARB: He may have told you that, but that shop actually belonged to someone else. He was just an employee there, too. And he didn't leave Tiffany's of his own volition. He was let go.

ANN ELIZA: Oh? Why?

MRS GOLDFARB: It seemed he was frequently absent.

ANN ELIZA: Oh, I know. He has these turns, you see. He disappeared from us from time to time, too.

MRS GOLDFARB: Well, what you don't know is the reason for his turns and the reason he was discharged from Tiffany's.

ANN ELIZA: No, why was that?

MRS GOLDFARB: This is difficult for me to say, I'm afraid.

ANN ELIZA: Please...tell me.

MRS GOLDFARB: Well, it seems that Mr. Ramy was terminated for drug taking. He was, as they told me, a capable workman, but they couldn't keep him straight.

ANN ELIZA is stricken at this news.

MRS GOLDFARB: I'm so sorry to have to tell you this, but you need to know it, especially since you're anxious about your sister.

ANN ELIZA: (*after a beat*) Oh, dear lord.

MRS GOLDFARB: (*patting her shoulder*) I'm so sorry.

ANN ELIZA: I...I had no idea.

MRS GOLDFARB: I'm sure it must be a terrible shock. If there's anything else I can do, please let me know.

ANN ELIZA: No, you done more than enough. Thank you for your help. (*indicating the dress*) I'll have this finished by tomorrow afternoon, like I said. If you want to send someone to pick it up then—or anytime really.

MRS GOLDFARB: I'll drop by myself. To see how you're doing.

ANN ELIZA still looks dazed.

MRS GOLDFARB: I'm so sorry.

ANN ELIZA: (*holding back tears*) Thank you. Thank you so much.

MRS GOLDFARB: (*at the door*) You're most welcome, Miss Bunner.

MRS GOLDFARB exis. ANN ELIZA stands motionless at the center of the room behind the half-wrapped clock. Her shock turning to anger, she looks down at the clock, lifts it into the air, and slams it down onto the floor, making a great sound, which reverberates louder and louder as the lights fade to black.

SCENE 2

A week or so later; late February. The lights come up on ANN ELIZA and MRS MELLINS in the living quarters. An open, half-packed suitcase sits on the bed. MRS MELLINS is finishing tea, while ANN ELIZA is up and down, pulling out and checking last-minute wardrobe possibilities.

ANN ELIZA: (*holding up an overcoat*) Sergeant Schultz says it's gonna be bitter out there. I hope this here one's warm enough.

MRS MELLINS: I can't believe you're going all the way out there by yourself.

ANN ELIZA: I can't neither—but Sergeant Schultz got me a boarding house that ain't too dear. I'm lucky Mrs. Goldfarb wanted two more little frocks.

MRS MELLINS: I still think you oughta hired a private

detective, like your sergeant said for you to do. And if they've got Pinkerton out there, they're the best. A lot of 'em have psychic powers, did you know that? I read where one of 'em found somebody in London and he never even had to set foot outta New York to do it.

ANN ELIZA: Rubbish.

MRS MELLINS: Believe what you like. It's the god's truth—I seen it in more than one magazine.

ANN ELIZA: Even if it is true, I could never afford one of them detectives. You know how much they charge? $20 a day. That's four times my train fare to St. Louis.

MRS MELLINS: Like I said before, if you could use a little help, I ain't got much to spare, but I could lend you a little...

ANN ELIZA: Thank you, Mrs. Mellins—but I ain't never borrowed money from no one—and I don't want to start.

MRS MELLINS: You're a stubborn one, Miss Bunner. (*a beat*) Do you really think you'll find her?

ANN ELIZA: I can only hope. My mother would never forgive me if I didn't try.

MRS MELLINS: What if you do find her and she won't come back?

ANN ELIZA: (*with resolve*) She will. I know in my heart that wherever she is, my sister's longing for me and longing to come back home.

MRS MELLINS: You see, you're still holding onto her. (*moving towards her*) Three months is a long time. And if you don't mind my saying so, I think you should be prepared for...

ANN ELIZA: For what?

MRS MELLINS: (*carefully*) The worst.

ANN ELIZA: You think I don't think about that every minute of the day? And if that's the case, if she is....*gone*, then at least I'll know. It's the not knowing that's killing me.

MRS MELLINS: I'm sorry, Miss Bunner—I just thought...

ANN ELIZA: I know—you've made your point. (*looking to where clock used to be*) What time is it?

MRS MELLINS: It was 11:30 when I came down. What time is your train?

ANN ELIZA: One o'clock. Mr. Hawkins is going to the station with me.

MRS MELLINS: Then I'd better leave you finish your packing. I'll be back before you set out. And I'm sorry about—

ANN ELIZA: *The worst*? Don't be. You meant well.

MRS MELLINS: Good day then, Miss Bunner.

ANN ELIZA: Good day, Mrs. Mellins.

MRS MELLINS exits as ANN ELIZA clears off the tea things and returns to packing her suitcase. After a long beat, she hears something at the door and then sees a dark figure standing outside trying to open it. ANN ELIZA walks cautiously toward the door and opens it slowly to reveal EVELINA. A shadow of her former self—wan, her hair straight and unwashed—she wears a shabby mantle under her now battered blue cape. ANN ELIZA is visibly shaken by the horror of EVELINA'S appearance.

ANN ELIZA: Sister...oh, Evelina! I knowed you'd come!

She pulls EVELINA to her. After letting herself be held for a beat, she draws back and looks around the shop.

EVELINA: I'm dead tired. Ain't there any fire?

ANN ELIZA: Of course there is.

ANN ELIZA takes her sister's hand and leads her into the living quarters, where she presses her into a chair.

ANN ELIZA: You're stone cold, ain't you? Just sit still and warm yourself while I get the kettle. I've got something you always used to fancy for supper.

EVELINA: I—I—

ANN ELIZA: (*trying to prolong the momentary joy of her sister's return*) Don't talk—oh, don't talk yet.

ANN ELIZA puts on the kettle, then brings a slice of custard pie from the cupboard to her sister.

ANN ELIZA: There, custard pie. You still like that, don't you? Mrs. Mellins just brought it down this morning. She had a couple of her granddaughters from New Jersey over to dinner last night. Ain't it funny it just so happened?

EVELINA: I ain't hungry. (*noticing that the clock is no longer on the shelf*) Where's the clock gone to?

ANN ELIZA: (*setting a teacup in front of EVELINA*) Oh, I—I gave that away. I gave it to Mrs. Hawkins. She's kept awake so many nights by that last baby.

EVELINA: Little Sheila?

ANN ELIZA: No, she's got another one already. Them Irish don't waste no time.

EVELINA: I wish you had never bought it.

ANN ELIZA starts to pour her a cup of tea; but she hesitates, puts down the teapot, and goes back to the cupboard where she takes out the cordial.

ANN ELIZA: Here, drink this right off—it'll warm you up quicker than anything. And besides, it's a special occasion.

EVELINA does as told and tries the pie as well. After just a bite, she lays down her fork.

EVELINA: I ain't hungry. I'm only so dead tired—that's the trouble.

ANN ELIZA: Then you'd better get right into bed. Here's my old plaid dressing gown—you remember it, don't you? The one you always kidded about for being old-fashioned?

ANN ELIZA gently undresses her sister, putting her into the dressing gown.

EVELINA: I've been to hell and back.

ANN ELIZA: Oh, Evelina—don't say it. Sister!

EVELINA: If I am back. It began right away, less than a month after we was married. I've been in hell all that time, Ann Eliza. (*a beat*) He took opium. I didn't find it out till long afterward. At first, when he acted so strange, I thought he drank. But it was worse, much worse than drinking.

ANN ELIZA: Oh, sister, don't say it—don't say it yet. It's so sweet just to have you here with me again.

EVELINA: I must say it. You don't know what life's like— you don't know anything about it—setting here safe all the while in this peaceful place.

ANN ELIZA: Oh, Evelina—why didn't you write and send for me if it was like that?

EVELINA: That's why I couldn't write. Didn't you guess I was ashamed.

ANN ELIZA: How could you be? Ashamed to write to Ann Eliza?

ANN ELIZA gets EVELINA into bed.

ANN ELIZA: Now lay down. You'll catch your death.

EVELINA: My death? That don't frighten me! You don't know what I've been through.

EVELINA arranges herself upright in bed to tell her story as ANN ELIZA takes off her shoes and rubs her feet.

EVELINA: The minute we got out there, and he found the job wasn't so good as he expected, he changed. He used to go off for hours at a time, and when he came back, his eyes kinder had a fog over them. Sometimes he didn't har'ly know me, and when he did, he seemed to hate me. Once he hit me here. (*indicates her breast*) Another time he disappeared for a whole ten days. They took him back at the store, and gave him another chance; but the second time, they discharged him for good. And when he found out about the baby—

ANN ELIZA: The baby?

EVELINA: It's dead—only lived a day. When he found out about it, he got mad, and said he hadn't any money to pay doctors' bills, and I'd better write to you to help us. He had an idea you had money hidden away that I didn't know about. It was him that made me get that extra hundred dollars outta you.

ANN ELIZA: Hush, hush. I always meant it for you anyhow.

EVELINA: Yes, but I wouldn't have taken it if he hadn't been at me the whole time. He used to make me do just what he wanted. And when I said I wouldn't write to you for more money, he said I'd better try and earn some myself. I tried to get work at a milliner's, but I was so sick I couldn't stay. I was sick all the time. I wisht I'd ha' died, Ann Eliza.

ANN ELIZA: No, no, Evelina.

EVELINA: When they turned us out because we couldn't pay the rent, we went to board with this German lady he knowed, a Mrs. Hochmüller. She wasn't bad to me, and I think she tried to keep him straight, but she had this daughter Linda— Anyway, I kep' getting worse, and he was always off for days at a time. The doctor had me sent to a hospital.

ANN ELIZA: A hospital! Sister...Sister!

EVELINA: It was better than being with him; and the doctors were real kind to me. And one day when I was laying there, Mrs. Hochmüller came in as white as a sheet, and told me him and Linda had gone off together and taken all her money. That's the last I ever saw of him.

She breaks off with a laugh, and then starts coughing.

ANN ELIZA: (*taking her sister's hand*) There, there. No more. Just lay down now, and sleep.

EVELINA: (*resisting*) When they left me out, I tried to find Mrs. Hochmüller, but she had moved. A lady visitor at the hospital found me a place where I did housework, but I was so weak, they couldn't keep me. After that, I begged in the streets.

ANN ELIZA: Oh, no. If our mother knew—

EVELINA: And one afternoon last week, when the matinees was coming out, I met a man with a pleasant face, and he stopped and asked me what the trouble was. I told him if he'd give me five dollars, I'd have money enough to buy a ticket back to New York. He took a good look at me and said, well, if that was what I wanted, he'd go straight to the station with me and give me the five dollars there. So he did—he bought the ticket and put me in the cars.

EVELINA sinks back into the pillows. The sisters hold each other without speaking. After a beat, the doorbell clangs. ANN ELIZA ignores it. The door opens and we see a dark figure cross the shop into the living quarters. It is MRS MELLINS.

MRS MELLINS: My sakes, Ann Eliza! What in the land are you doing? Miss Evelina—Mrs. Ramy—it ain't you?

ANN ELIZA: My sister Evelina has come back—come back on a visit. She was taken sick in the cars on the way home—I guess she caught cold—so I made her go right to bed. Mr. Ramy has gone west on a trip—at trip connected with his business—and Evelina is going to stay with me till he comes back.

MRS MELLINS: (*baffled*) Well, welcome back, dearie. I'll come back and see you when you're feeling better.

ANN ELIZA: (*to MRS MELLINS*) Yes, tomorrow will be better. Right now, my dear little sister needs to sleep.

MRS MELLINS: Why, yes. Of course. If there's anything I can do—

ANN ELIZA: Not now. But thank you. She'll be fine. (*to EVELINA*) Won't you, my sweet Evelina? Everything's gonna be all right—now that you're back home.

MRS MELLINS stands looking at the two sisters as the clock ticks and the lights fade to black.

SCENE 3

About a week has passed; it is morning, early March.
EVELINA is motionless in bed in the living quarters, which are
in half-light, whereas ANN ELIZA is in the shop, which is fully
lit, working on another child's dress. She looks up and sees
MRS MELLINS coming down the outside stairs to the shop.
She puts the dress aside and opens the door for her neighbor.

MRS MELLINS: I seen the doctor leaving. How is she? What did he say?

ANN ELIZA: She ain't no better.

MRS MELLINS: What is it? Pneumonia I reckon.

ANN ELIZA: Well, I might as well tell you. It's worse.

MRS MELLINS: Not consumption?

ANN ELIZA: He wants to put her in St. Luke's.

MRS MELLINS: When?

ANN ELIZA: Now. But I want to keep her here. It won't make much difference one way or t'other.

MRS MELLINS: Is she gonna—

ANN ELIZA: They won't tell you that. I asked him. He just said "human skill works wonders."

MRS MELLINS: Oh, dear me. (*sits at the work table*) You know my own sister took sick a couple of years ago and she got treated by this doctor that specialized in—

ANN ELIZA: Not now, Mrs. Mellins. I ain't got time for no stories now. I gotta ask you something important though.

MRS MELLINS: What's that, Miss Bunner?

ANN ELIZA: That there doctor—his services ain't free. Remember last week you offered to lend me some—for a detective? Well, things is changed and—

MRS MELLINS: You want me to lend it to you? Why of course, Miss Bunner.

ANN ELIZA: I'll have it back to you next week, when Mrs. Goldfarb picks up another of them little dresses.

MRS MELLINS: Honest, I'm happy to.

ANN ELIZA: Thank you, Mrs. Mellins.

MRS MELLINS: (*a beat*) I guess you ain't had any news from *him*.

ANN ELIZA: You would be referring to Ramy?

MRS MELLINS: I would indeed. Does he know how sick she is?

ANN ELIZA: He don't know nuttin'.

MRS MELLINS: But shouldn't you tell him? When's he back from his business trip out West?

ANN ELIZA: (*with difficulty*) Mrs. Mellins—I can't keep it from you no longer.

MRS MELLINS: What?

ANN ELIZA: I made up that story. The truth is Ramy walked out on Evelina months ago—and she ain't heard a word from him ever since.

MRS MELLINS: That scoundrel!

ANN ELIZA: He was a liar—about everything. I shoudda realized it.

MRS MELLINS: Men—they're all liars.

ANN ELIZA: Do you know the real reason for all a them "turns" of his?

MRS MELLINS: No, what?

ANN ELIZA: He's a drug fiend!

MRS MELLINS: (*shocked but titillated by this revelation*) No! How'd you find that out?

ANN ELIZA: His old boss at Tiff'ny's told Mrs. Goldfarb.

MRS MELLINS: Well, that don't surprise me. I never trusted that man from the beginning.

ANN ELIZA: Whether you trusted him or not, he's turned out to be just like some of them people you read about in your magazines.

MRS MELLINS: Poor girl. Poor, poor girl.

ANN ELIZA: And here I am—borrowing money for the first time in my life—and turning into a lair myself. How did it come to this, Mrs. Mellins? How?

MRS MELLINS: The Lord sometimes gives us a lot to endure. He tests us in strange ways.

ANN ELIZA: I used to think that, too. But I ain't so sure I believe it anymore. I always thought everything I did for Evelina—and everything I gave up for myself—was for her happiness. And I always trusted in the goodness of God to reward me for doing my duty. I just don't know anymore. I don't know what I trust. Who I believe. What I believe. It's like a big black cloud hanging over the Bunner sisters.

MRS MELLINS: Oh, Miss Bunner. You mustn't think like that. You mustn't lose faith. If we ain't got that, we ain't got nuttin'.

ANN ELIZA: I know—that's a frightening thought, ain't it?

A faint call of "Sister" and then a loud fit of coughing issue from the other room.

ANN ELIZA: Oh, dear. I'm sorry to burden you with all this Mrs. Mellins. Excuse me. I'd better go see to her.

MRS MELLINS: Can I go in?

ANN ELIZA: Not with her coughing like that. Best wait till she's more comfortable. The doctor gave me some extra-strong medicine.

MRS MELLINS: Of course, I understand. And don't you worry about that money. I'll get it to you right away.

ANN ELIZA: Thank you, Mrs. Mellins.

MRS MELLINS exits and ANN ELIZA goes into the living quarters, picking up a bottle of cough syrup and a spoon from the cupboard. She approaches EVELINA in bed, offering her a spoonful of the medicine.

ANN ELIZA: Here, here. The doctor said this would help.

EVELINA swallows it with difficulty; her cough does begin to subside.

EVELINA: What else did the doctor say?

ANN ELIZA doesn't answer.

EVELINA: He must a said something. What was it?

ANN ELIZA: Why, he said you'd have to be careful—and stay in bed—and take this new medicine I just give you.

EVELINA: Did he say I was going to get well?

ANN ELIZA: Why, Evelina!

EVELINA: What's the use, Ann Eliza? You can't deceive me. I seen myself in the glass earlier. I seen plenty of 'em in the hospital that looked like me. They didn't get well, and I ain't going to. (*her head dropping back on the pillows*) It don't much matter—I'm about tired. Only there's one thing. There's one thing I ain't told you. I didn't want to tell you yet because I was afraid you might be sorry—but if he says I'm going to die, I've got to say it.

She beings to cough.

ANN ELIZA: Don't talk now—you're tired.

EVELINA: I'll be tired-er tomorrow, I guess. And I want you should know. Sit down close to me.

ANN ELIZA moves closer to her on the bed and strokes her hand.

EVELINA: I'm a Roman Catholic, Ann Eliza.

ANN ELIZA: What? Oh, Evelina—Evelina Bunner! A Roman Catholic, you? Oh, Evelina, did *he* make you?

EVELINA: Him? Naw! I guess he didn't have no religion. He never spoke of it. But you see, Mrs. Hochmüller was a Catholic and so when I was sick she got the doctor to send me to a Roman Catholic hospital and the sisters was so good to me there—and the priest used to come and talk to me...and the things he told me kept me from going crazy. He seemed to make everything easier.

ANN ELIZA: But, sister—how could you? Go over to the Papists?

EVELINA: And then when the baby was born—over three months early—he christened it right away, so it could go to heaven, and after that, you see, I had to be a Catholic—

ANN ELIZA: I don't see—

ANN ELIZA slowly draws her hand away from EVELINA.

EVELINA: Don't I have to be where the baby is? I couldn't ever ha' gone there if I hadn't been made a Catholic. Don't you understand that?

ANN ELIZA doesn't answer.

EVELINA: I've got to go where the baby is. (*taking her hand*) If I get worse, I want you to send for a priest. Mrs. Mellins'll know where to find one. Promise me faithful you will.

ANN ELIZA: (*after a beat*) Yes...I promise.

Slow fade to black against the sound of a Gregorian requiem chant.

SCENE 4

A week later. A PRIEST is sitting in a chair beside Evelina in bed. The stage is dimly lit. As he gives her Communion, he recites the following:

PRIEST: This is the Lamb of God, that takest away the sins of the world. Happy are those who are called to his supper. (*softly to Evelina*) Now repeat after me: Oh Lord, I am not worthy to receive Thee...

EVELINA: (*softly*) Oh Lord, I am not worthy to receive Thee...

PRIEST: Say but the word and my soul shall be healed...

EVELINA: Say but the word and my soul shall be healed...

The priest now anoints EVELINA'S forehead with oil from a small vial.

PRIEST: Through this holy anointing, may the Lord, in his love and mercy, help you with the grace of the Holy Spirit. May the Lord, who frees you from sin, save you and raise you up.

The lights come up stage left, to reveal ANN ELIZA and MRS MELLINS sitting quietly.

MRS MELLINS: It's gone awful quiet in there. You think we should go in?

ANN ELIZA: No, I don't want no part in any of them secret ceremonies.

MRS MELLINS: She'd just be making her confession and he'd be praying for her soul to go to heaven.

ANN ELIZA: And you don't need priests or ceremonies for any of that. Our mother would be rolling over in her grave if she knew—

MRS MELLINS: Well, she don't know. If it comforts your sister, why do you care?

ANN ELIZA: You're right, Mrs. Mellins. I just gotta stop fussing about it. It ain't none of my business how Evelina wants to die. But all this Catholic business—I guess I just feel...a little left out.

MRS MELLINS: It ain't between you and Evelina no more. It's between her and the Lord.

ANN ELIZA sighs as the PRIEST leaves the back room and comes into the shop.

MRS MELLINS: How is she, Father?

ANN ELIZA: Yes, tell us, sir. Please.

PRIEST: I have left your sister in a very beautiful state of mind. She is full of spiritual consolation.

ANN ELIZA is silent.

MRS MELLINS: Thank you, Father.

ANN ELIZA: Yes...thank you.

PRIEST: You will let me know when—

ANN ELIZA: Yes, we will.

PRIEST: May God bless you.

MRS MELLINS: I'll leave you alone with her. Come up and fetch me if you need to.

ANN ELIZA: Thank you, Mrs. Mellins. I will.

MRS MELLINS exits with the PRIEST, as ANN ELIZA moves slowly into the living quarters, where she kneels beside her sister, taking her hand. EVELINA is in a state of ecstasy. She smiles at her sister.

EVELINA: Oh, sister...

ANN ELIZA: Yes, I'm here.

EVELINA: Oh, sister. I...I shall see the baby.

She falls back against the pillows and closes her eyes. ANN ELIZA remains on her knees, holding her sister's hand. The lights fade slowly as we again hear the requiem chant.

SCENE 5

Two weeks later. Lights come up on the shop and living quarters. The shelves are bare; the front display windows are stripped of their artificial flowers, hat frames, and limp garments. Against the glass pane of the doorway hangs a sign (which we see in reverse) "Store to Let". A few boxes are stacked on and next to the worktable, where ANN ELIZA and MRS MELLINS are engaged in packing them.

ANN ELIZA: (*holding up the dress EVELINA wore for her outing with MR RAMY in Central Park*) I made this special for her—she looked so lovely that day.

MRS MELLINS: Are you gonna keep it?

ANN ELIZA puts the dress on the mannequin.

ANN ELIZA: Of course. I want to remember her when she was young and pretty.

MRS MELLINS: All you have to do is close your eyes and you can see her that way. You don't need no dress for that.

ANN ELIZA: Then, what do you suggest I do with it?

MRS MELLINS: Take it off that dummy and give it to someone who will use it and enjoy it. I bet it would fit the oldest Hawkins girl—if not now, then soon.

ANN ELIZA: That's a good thought, Mrs. Mellins. But I'd like to keep her here just a little bit longer.

MRS MELLINS: Suit yourself. I can't believe you're leaving us, Ann Eliza. Are you sure you got to?

ANN ELIZA: With the business falling off so bad, I ain't got no choice. I can't live on making Mrs. Goldfarb a children's party dress from time to time.

MRS MELLINS: We'll miss you. You'll have to visit us as often as you can.

ANN ELIZA: Oh, I will.

MRS MELLINS: Too bad you didn't get that saleslady job up on the Square.

ANN ELIZA: They wanted somebody younger. I've been hearing that a lot.

MRS MELLILNS: Well, don't let it get you down.

ANN ELIZA: The worst thing is gonna be living in a boarding house. I swore when Evelina and I moved in here, we'd never board again. And we both wound up doing it, her in St. Louis and now me here.

MRS MELLINS: You're sure there's no way you can stay on?

ANN ELIZA: No. Besides, there's too many memories here—good and bad.

MRS MELLINS: You'll get over the bad ones.

ANN ELIZA: I don't know, Mrs. Mellins. Anyway, I think we've packed enough for today. I got an appointment at that new jewelry store up on 23rd Street. They're looking for salesladies. I'm gonna start looking into sewing factories, too. I guess I ain't too old for sitting at a sewing machine 14 hours a day.

MRS MELLINS: Oh, Lord. We can't let you—

ANN ELIZA: I don't have no choice.

The doorbell clangs.

ANN ELIZA: I wonder who that could be. Maybe somebody wants to let the shop.

Ann Eliza walks to the door to admit MRS GOLDFARB.

ANN ELIZA: Mrs. Goldfarb—

MRS GOLDFARB: I'm glad I found you in. When I saw the "To Let" sign, I thought you might have gone already.

ANN ELIZA: Oh, no. I'm here a couple more days.

MRS GOLDFARB: I wanted to extend my condolences in person.

ANN ELIZA: We sure appreciated the flowers.

MRS GOLDFARB: I'm glad you liked them.

MRS MELLINS: Yes, it was the biggest bouquet in the whole cemetery.

MRS GOLDFARB: (*slightly embarrassed*) Ah, well…thank you, dear.

MRS MELLINS: And I was just leaving, so if you ladies will excuse me.

ANN ELIZA: Thank you, Mrs. Mellins—for your help with the packing.

MRS MELLINS: Think nothing of it. Goodbye, ladies.

MRS GOLDFARB nods goodbye as MRS MELLINS exits.

MRS GOLDFARB: Well, I'm sure you're very busy, Miss Bunner. I won't keep you.

ANN ELIZA: Please, Mrs. Goldfarb. Can I get you a cup a tea?

MRS GOLDFARB: No, thank you. I can't stay long. (*noticing the mannequin with EVELINA'S dress*) Lovely dress.

ANN ELIZA: It was my sister's. You must recognize the sleeves.

MRS GOLDFARB: Oh, I do. Of course now everybody's wearing them.

ANN ELIZA: (*indicates a stool*) Please, sit down for a minute.

MRS GOLDFARB: (*sits*) I understand you're looking for a job.

ANN ELIZA: (*sitting*) I am. Without Evelina, I can't keep the shop going on my own, so I've been looking for sales work on the outside. But there ain't much out there for a 40-year-old woman, so I'm about to look into the sewing factories.

MRS GOLDFARB: You mean the sweatshops.

ANN ELIZA: I guess you could call 'em that—but we gotta work where the work is.

MRS GOLDFARB: Miss Bunner, I've been thinking a lot about something.

ANN ELIZA: What was that, Mrs. Goldfarb?

MRS GOLDFARB: Well, these little dresses you've been making for me and my circle.

ANN ELIZA: Yes? I'm glad you like them.

MRS GOLDFARB: Everybody likes them—adores them in fact. Why, right now, I have another friend who wants one for her niece.

ANN ELIZA: Oh, well, I guess I could run up one more—as I ain't found a job yet.

MRS GOLDFARB: I'm not thinking about just one.

ANN ELIZA: What do you mean?

MRS GOLDFARB: I was thinking of a whole collection.

ANN ELIZA: I'm sorry, I don't understand.

MRS GOLDFARB: A whole collection of party dresses for little girls based on the latest styles from Paris.

ANN ELIZA: What are you saying?

MRS GOLDFARB: I'm saying I'd like to start a business.

ANN ELIZA: A business?

MRS GOLDFARB: Yes, but I can't do it alone. I need help.

ANN ELIZA: What kind of help?

MRS GOLDFARB: An expert seamstress. Someone who knows how fabrics fit together...someone who knows how to make something beautiful. Someone like you.

ANN ELIZA: (*a beat*) Me? A business? Why I couldn't do that—I ain't had the experience.

MRS GOLDFARB: What do you mean? You've been running

a business here for—I don't know—how many years?

ANN ELIZA: Twelve.

MRS GOLDFARB: Well, I'd call that a lot of experience.

ANN ELIZA: But it was my sister did all the fancy work.

MRS GOLDFARB: You're selling yourself short—you did
most of the children's dresses all by yourself.

ANN ELIZA: With a little help from Mrs. Mellins upstairs.

MRS GOLDFARB: So you can hire her. Once we get going,
you may need to hire even more seamstresses.

ANN ELIZA: (*not convinced*) It would be a big responsibility.
I ain't sure I'm up to it—especially with Evelina gone and all.

MRS GOLDFARB: You don't have to decide now—but think
about it.

ANN ELIZA: Yes, I will. (*a beat*) Mrs. Goldfarb?

MRS GOLDFARB: Yes?

ANN ELIZA: Thank you. For even considering me. But I just
don't think I'm up to it.

MRS GOLDFARB: I'd still like you to think long and hard
about it. I realize it's a big risk. For both of us. My husband
thinks I'm crazy. Women aren't supposed to run businesses.
I'd like to prove him wrong. We don't know where it might
lead. I could lose all my investment. But for you, a job in a
sewing factory—where would that lead? What kind of life
would that be? Living in a boarding house and mourning the
loss of your sister for the rest of your days? Your sister is
gone, Miss Bunner. She's as dead as that mannequin over

there—and nothing can bring her back. But you're still alive. Yes, it is a huge risk and a huge responsibility, I grant you that, but it's a huge opportunity too.

ANN ELIZA: (*a beat*) I don't know. I just don't know, Mrs. Goldfarb.

MRS GOLDFARB: As I said, you don't have to make up your mind immediately. But please do think about it.

ANN ELIZA: Yes. I will...of course I will.

MRS GOLDFARB: And again, my condolences. I know that this is a difficult time for you and I don't want to make it any more so. Good-day, Miss Bunner.

ANN ELIZA: Good-day, Mrs. Goldfarb.

MRS GOLDFARB exits. ANN ELIZA stands motionless for a beat, then goes to the coat rack and puts on her coat and bonnet. As she does this, her eyes fall on the "To Let" sign. She takes it off the door, looks at it, and then turns to take in the shop, EVELINA'S dress, and the living area. Ultimately she stares straight out as the lights come down slowly until only her face is illuminated. We hear the same 1880s New York City street noises that we heard at the beginning of the play. The light on Ann Eliza fades to black.

CURTAIN

END OF PLAY

ACKNOWLEDGMENTS

Many thanks to my old college friend and fellow playwright Chalmers Hardenbergh, who encouraged me to stop talking about *The Bunner Sisters* and start writing. Thanks, too, to my partner Anthony Newfield, who stood by me while I was writing and who convinced me, when I had my doubts, that I had a play. This was confirmed when we had our first reading for a few friends at the Irish Repertory Theatre, who generously allowed us to use their space. The audience reaction was decidedly positive; the play needed work, of course, but everyone was enthusiastic about the play's potential. Over the next two years, we had more readings—honing, cutting, adding new scenes, taking out others. I can't thank enough all the fine actors who lent their time and their talent during this period: Charlotte Maier, Annette Hunt, Alan Coates, Joan Juliet Buck, Stephanie Janssen, Linda Atkinson, Jill Larson, Polly McKie, Rachel Pickup, Delphi Harrington, Anthony Crane, Lee Aaron Rosen, Adrea Vitlar, Julia Gibson, Joy Carlin, Nancy Carlin, Cathleen Riddley, Elena Wright, and Carole Monferdini. I am also grateful to the multi-talented Steven Carl McCasland for his handsome cover design and for his help in getting the Bunners into print. Finally, huge thanks go to Josiah Polhemus and Amy Prosser of RE:ACT, the bold little theater company in San Francisco that liked *The Bunner Sisters* well enough to take a chance on it and actually produce it. Directed by Anthony Newfield, it was a classy production with a fine set by Jessica Bertine, gorgeous period costumes by Chanterelle Grover, and stellar performances from actors Josiah Pohemus, Amy Prosser, Heather Kellogg, Anne Buelteman, and Tara Blau. And one more thank you: Edith Wharton, who I felt was looking over my shoulder as I adapted her beautiful language and compelling story from page to stage. Thank you, Mrs. Wharton.

ABOUT THE AUTHOR

Richard Alleman has written for American *Vogue* for over three decades, where he was the magazine's long-time Travel Editor. He has also written for *The Economist*, British and German *Vogue*s, *Travel + Leisure, Condé Nast Traveler, In-Style,* and *Milieu.* He is the author of the classic guidebooks *Hollywood: A Movie Lover's Guide* and *New York: A Movie Lover's Guide* (Random House/Broadway Books), which he recently updated for their electronic editions. He co-wrote the screenplay for the film *Casa Hollywood*, and his play *Scenario of Death* was produced Off-Broadway at the Nat Horn Theatre. Based in London from 1998 to 2008, Alleman worked as an actor on both stage and television. His favorite role was that of an aging Tom Cruise in several episodes of Armando Iannucci's BBC comedy series *Time Trumpet.* He holds a BA in Drama from the University of California, Berkeley.